W9-BSG-879

NEW ESSAYS ON RABBIT, RUN

Still John Updike's most popular and critically acclaimed novel, *Rabbit, Run* was written in 1959 when the author was only twenty-eight years old; it announced the thematic concerns and stylistic innovations through which the author was to explore the American psyche and gauge the temper and history of its culture over the next three decades. The first of a tetralogy, *Rabbit, Run* introduced the character of Harry "Rabbit" Angstrom, one of those middle-class Americans who, in Updike's view, aren't especially beautiful or bright or urban but about whom there is a lot worth saying. The fallible hero struggles with his own sexuality, his religious feelings, the difficulties of being a son and a father, and with the changes in American society that confuse and excite, and finally seem to suffocate him. Updike's writing is charged with narrative energy and pictorial accuracy that illuminate the present moment as they evoke the tension between the drab compromises we are forced to make with age and the religious mystery that sustains us against them. Written by a distinguished group of international scholars, the essays in this collection examine both the technical mastery and thematic range that make this work one of the most significant achievements in modern American fiction and one which continues to provoke fresh critical insight.

★ The American Novel ★

GENERAL EDITOR
Emory Elliott
University of California, Riverside

Other books in the series:
New Essays on The Scarlet Letter
New Essays on The Great Gatsby
New Essays on Adventures of Huckleberry Finn
New Essays on Moby-Dick
New Essays on Uncle Tom's Cabin
New Essays on The Red Badge of Courage
New Essays on The Sun Also Rises
New Essays on A Farewell to Arms
New Essays on The American
New Essays on The Portrait of a Lady
New Essays on Light in August
New Essays on The Awakening
New Essays on Invisible Man
New Essays on Native Son
New Essays on Their Eyes Were Watching God
New Essays on The Grapes of Wrath
New Essays on Winesburg, Ohio
New Essays on Sister Carrie
New Essays on The Rise of Silas Lapham
New Essays on The Catcher in the Rye
New Essays on White Noise
New Essays on The Crying of Lot 49
New Essays on Walden
New Essays on Poe's Major Tales
New Essays on Hawthorne's Major Tales
New Essays on Daisy Miller and The Turn of the Screw
New Essays on The Sound and the Fury

New Essays on Rabbit, Run

Edited by
Stanley Trachtenberg

CAMBRIDGE UNIVERSITY PRESS

Published by the Press Syndicate of the University of Cambridge
The Pitt Building, Trumpington Street, Cambridge CB2 1RP
40 West 20th Street, New York, NY 10011-4211, USA
10 Stamford Road, Oakleigh, Melbourne 3166, Australia

First published 1993

Printed in the United States of America

Library of Congress Cataloging-in-Publication Data

New essays on Rabbit, run / edited by Stanley Trachtenberg.
p. cm. – (The American novel)
Includes bibliographical references.
ISBN 0-521-43337-1. – ISBN 0-521-43884-5 (pbk.)
1. Updike, John. Rabbit, run. 2. Angstrom, Harry (Fictitious character) I. Trachtenberg, Stanley. II. Series.
PS3571.P4R335 1993
813′.54 – dc20 93-21806

A catalog record for this book is available from the British Library.

ISBN 0–521–43337–1 hardback
ISBN 0–521–43884–5 paperback

Contents

Series Editor's Preface

In literary criticism the last twenty-five years have been particularly fruitful. Since the rise of the New Criticism in the 1950s, which focused attention of critics and readers upon the text itself – apart from history, biography, and society – there has emerged a wide variety of critical methods which have brought to literary works a rich diversity of perspectives: social, historical, political, psychological, economic, ideological, and philosophical. While attention to the text itself, as taught by the New Critics, remains at the core of contemporary interpretation, the widely shared assumption that works of art generate many different kinds of interpretations has opened up possibilities for new readings and new meanings.

Before this critical revolution, many works of American literature had come to be taken for granted by earlier generations of readers as having an established set of recognized interpretations. There was a sense among many students that the canon was established and that the larger thematic and interpretative issues had been decided. The task of the new reader was to examine the ways in which elements such as structure, style, and imagery contributed to each novel's acknowledged purpose. But recent criticism has brought these old assumptions into question and has thereby generated a wide variety of original, and often quite surprising, interpretations of the classics, as well as of rediscovered works such as Kate Chopin's *The Awakening*, which has only recently entered the canon of works that scholars and critics study and that teachers assign their students.

The aim of The American Novel Series is to provide students of American literature and culture with introductory critical guides to American novels and other important texts now widely read and studied. Usually devoted to a single work, each volume begins with an introduction by the volume editor, a distinguished authority on the text. The introduction presents details of the work's composition, publication history, and contemporary reception, as well as a survey of the major critical trends and readings from first publication to the present. This overview is followed by four or five original essays, specifically commissioned from senior scholars of established reputation and from outstanding younger critics. Each essay presents a distinct point of view, and together they constitute a forum of interpretative methods and of the best contemporary ideas on each text.

It is our hope that these volumes will convey the vitality of current critical work in American literature, generate new insights and excitement for students of American literature, and inspire new respect for and new perspectives upon these major literary texts.

Emory Elliott
University of California, Riverside

1

Introduction

STANLEY TRACHTENBERG

WRITTEN in 1959 when Updike was only twenty-eight and published by Knopf one year later, *Rabbit, Run*, Updike's second novel, was still the one he was best known by the author somewhat ruefully remarked nearly twenty years after its publication. By the end of the first year, it had sold more than twenty thousand copies. To date, including paperback editions that have gone through over fifty printings, the figure has climbed to more than 2.5 million.[1] Updike acknowledged the book was written with no thought of a sequel and only after some experiments with an autobiographical poem, "Midpoint," and a play about James Buchanan did he decide to return to the novel form. The agitation of the sixties persuaded him that "Rabbit Angstrom of Pennsylvania, about whose future some people had expressed curiosity, might be the vehicle in which to package some of the American unease that was ranging all around us."[2]

Updike has indicated that his initial intention was to contrast *Rabbit, Run* with a companion novella, *The Centaur*, both to be published in a single volume, one novel illustrating a more responsible pattern of behavior, the other more that of instinctual gratification.[3] The rabbit book proved too large to include with that of the horse and the compelling force exerted on Updike's imagination by its central character is evidenced by the three other books he has written at roughly ten-year intervals chronicling Rabbit's adventures, increasingly a mirror of the time and place in which they occur. Yet though *Rabbit, Run* reflected the Eisenhower era, or perhaps because of it, its emphasis was at least as much on Rabbit's struggle to liberate himself from the sexual customs and social attitudes of the period as on its history. Like the writers of the fifties, Updike explained, he tried to find excitement in the normal, everyday life, "the quality of things at rest." Accordingly, he focused "on investigation of the quotidian, whereas the generations older and younger than mine have been more economic and political in their orientations."[4]

The novel was written in pencil, then typed by the author, in a second-story corner room of a house in Ipswich, Massachusetts, to which, supported in part by a grant from the Guggenheim Foundation, he had moved his family after giving up a job with the *New Yorker* he had held for two years. Although somewhat removed from the scene of the novel, Updike nonetheless called attention to the fact that it was written coterminously with the public events it depicted. Updike described its structure as a zigzag pattern, reflecting the motions of a rabbit, motions his hero duplicated, but the book was written consecutively. "I have never made it my habit to skip a scene and then come back to it," Updike has explained. "You are in danger of losing the music, or the thread, in that way."[5] Some episodes did disturb Updike, however. He was concerned about the scene in which Janice drowns the baby, which was composed in what he describes as a little hot attic room at his then wife's parents' summer place in Vermont. "I wrote all day, smoking profusely, and when I came down at tea-time, dizzy with nicotine and vicarious anguish, I announced, 'I killed the baby.' "[6]

With *Rabbit, Run* Updike moved beyond the brilliant promise of *The Poorhouse Fair,* and looking back, he may have felt as though all his work from then on was judged against this second novel. Despite widespread acclaim for the precision of the language and for its evocative power, initial response to the novel was decidedly mixed. Stanley Edgar Hyman remarked on the author's intelligence, learning, honesty, and creative imagination, and regarded him as "the most gifted young writer in America." David Boroff in *The New York Times* found the subject "the stuff of shabby domestic tragedy," and its milieu one of spiritual poverty in which "the old people are listless and defeated, the young mostly empty." Even Boroff, however, noted that the unusually graphic treatment of sex revealed something of "the erotic sophistication of the postwar generation."[7]

Reviewers seemed offended, not, as might have been expected, by the explicit sexuality, but by the character of the central figure, by the fact that the author seemed neutral toward his self-indulgence, and by the consequent ambivalent ending of the novel. Taking note of the inconclusive ending, Richard Gilman placed the novel in the tradition of French antiliterature associated with Alain Robbe-Grillet or Nathalie Sarraute and described *Rabbit, Run* as a "grotesque allegory of American life with its myth of happiness and success." Although acknowledging Harry's less than admirable character, Gilman regarded the book as a "minor epic of the spirit thirsting for room to discover and *be* itself, ducking, dodging, staying out of reach of everything that will pin it down and impale it on fixed, immutable laws that are not of its own making and do not consider its integrity."[8]

Another reviewer, Milton Rugoff, was far more critical. Rugoff saw in Rabbit a complex of vague ideals and uncontrolled desires, as lacking in distinction as the vulgar and tasteless life he is running from. Though Rugoff placed the novel in the tradition of Dreiser's *An American Tragedy,* he regarded Rabbit's rebellion as perverse, limited to a nostalgic longing for former athletic triumphs. Accordingly, Rugoff felt Rabbit was as much responsible for his fate as its victim and termed the entire novel compressed even to the point of being hallucinatory.[9]

Writing in the *Partisan Review,* John Thompson not surprisingly objected as much to the world he found in Updike's novel as to the lack of compassion the author adopted in describing it. He termed Updike's style ultimately revolting for its indiscriminate application of heightened imagery, both to Rabbit's inchoate feelings and to the more neutral narrative passages. As a result, Thompson concluded, obvious truths about the period were mixed with covert meanings about the squalor of life and authenticity of feeling was identified with the impulse of death.[10]

In contrast, George Steiner described Updike as a new and powerful voice of the mid-fifties, cosmopolitan and nonchalant and resonant of both Joyce and Nabokov. Steiner, however, also thought the book "faintly precious, faintly cruel." Pointing to what he described as a "faintly shopworn air" that hovered over the central action of an ex-athlete unable to adjust to the loss of his former glory, Steiner complained of the absence of an ironic distancing, affording an undoubted directness and intensity but not providing a means to assess what the reader experiences. Steiner nonetheless found *Rabbit, Run* to be a fascinating novel, redeemed by passages of striking language and invested with an integrity that makes use of pervasive and explicit sexuality to break out of the deadening conformity of the American middle-class existence.[11]

Style, perhaps predictably, was the focus of a more favorable review by Whitney Balliett in the *New Yorker.* He felt that Updike's poetic but unobtrusive writing created a new prose of "precision, freshness, and grace" that set up a verbal rather than a narrative tension. Though Balliett, too, thought Updike cast a cold eye on humanity, whose failure to meet his high moral standards led him to "write *at* his characters," the tone was seen less as an expression of full-fledged misanthropy than as one of uncompromising indignation.[12]

Time magazine saw less of that sustaining value. The author's attempt to show what much of life in the United States was like, the reviewer contended, resulted in a depressing and frequently sordid story whose hero was a "weak, sensual, selfish and confused moral bankrupt" devoid of inner resources. Reflecting the more fastidious morality of the times, *Time* disapprovingly concluded that the novel contained "such relentless despair as is seldom found in U.S. writing" and though the reviewer acknowledged that it was in places commandingly written, its principal importance was said to lie mainly in shock value.[13]

The *Time* review was accompanied by a photo of a youthful Updike posed against a bookshelf, looking up from a book he holds open and during perusal of which he seems to have been interrupted. In this literary pose the *Time* writer saw a resemblance to the sober manner of Picasso's *Boy Leading a Horse.* Updike, however, looks at the photographer with a sly, slightly crooked grin that suggests he is too shrewd to believe what is being said about him but too polite to say so. The ambiguity of his expression seems to echo his stated reluctance to identify Rabbit as a representative American figure and his insistence on a "certain necessary ambiguity" in the novel which he did not wish "to be any clearer than life."

Overseas the reviews were even less receptive. An unsigned review in the London *Times Literary Supplement* found Updike's theme of delayed adolescence to accurately reflect contemporary American reality. Updike's acute observation of domestic social scenes, however, seemed to the reviewer balanced by the author's tendency to overwrite, so that the expressive brilliance of individual passages was diminished by the cumulative effect of the prose. For the critic in the *New Statesman*, what promised to be a fierce attack on lower middle-class life inside America was weakened by the book's "introspective brooding and interminable sex." Olivia Manning in *The Spectator* similarly complained of Updike's "philosophical musings, turgid thought-processes, and those inevitable sex passages which, so often repeated, are becoming as stimulating to the normal reader as posting a letter." In short, Manning concluded, *Rabbit, Run* was a "pretty much up-to-the-minute American novel."[14] These judgments were echoed by Anthony Burgess who acknowledged that despite being both young and American Updike had already given evidence of "those qualities which Europeans still think they monopolize – fastidiousness, Flaubertian martyrdom, an innocent belief in the power of exact language." Nonetheless Burgess contended that *Rabbit, Run* lacked both irony or social criticism in dealing with the trivial lives it delineated.[15]

Updike revised the novel four years after it came out, principally, he explained, to restore some of the more explicit sexual passages Knopf's legal department had asked him to delete. These and subsequent revisions Updike made in the text were also intended to sharpen the thematic definition as well as clarify the meaning. Above all, perhaps, they emphasized the graphic quality of his prose, a quality suggested by the subtitle penciled in but later deleted from the original manuscript: "A Motion Picture."[16]

Updike has acknowledged the influence of film in eliminating the authorial voice in the novel and so providing an altered sense of space, and in giving him the idea of what a story was and so developing narration as a fictive device. "In movies," he explained,

> something makes it entrance onto the screen and the viewer doesn't know how it came in, nor does he feel he needs to have it explained. The movie has the strangeness of a natural landscape. Nothing seems to have been created; it just happens to be there.[17]

Updike created this landscape in *Rabbit, Run* through the use of the present tense to correspond to the continuous present of movies and by the omission of time-bridging paragraphs. The opening scene of boys playing basketball was, he told one interviewer, intended to serve as a background against which the title and credits of a film could be projected.[18] At the same time Updike expressed some reservations about imitating the instantaneity of film in the novelist's art, a method resulting in an account, he speculated, the authority of which may have been diminished with the loss of the "presiding, talkative, confiding, and pedagogic author."[19]

The visual emphasis of the film approach suggests the animating impulse of the novel is a desire to render the texture of immediate experience at least as much as to record the social background out of which it emerges or even to see the destiny of the characters in terms of the conflict shaped by that background. When, in 1970, the novel was made into a movie, extraordinary care was taken to ensure fidelity to the original. Duplicating the book almost scene by scene the screenwriter called his script a "transcription" rather than a screenplay, and Updike himself commented on the "evident respect for the book" the movie displayed, calling it

> a brave picture that does attempt to take us into a real middle America and not a caricature, that does try to cope with how much of our lives happens below the belt, and which has many scenes that will be permanently imprinted on my brain.[20]

Universally condemned by the critics and unsuccessful at the box office (even the actress who played the role of Rabbit's wife criticized it), the film was updated from the fifties to the sixties and thus lacked the context of the deadening Eisenhower years which gave point to Rabbit's need to rebel. The motivation for Rabbit's behavior then becomes personal, almost an expression of petulance rather than a reaction to constricting social pressure. The movie thus misses the novel's ambivalance toward Rabbit and, in particular, its sympathy for his desire to escape the trap of middle-class conformity. Subsequently Updike acknowledged that the movie failed in a number of ways, one of which was precisely in its attempt at literal fidelity at the expense of the novel's underlying spirit. As a result, Updike noted, "they produced an enigmatic version of what is very clear in the book."[21]

As well as film, Updike acknowledged the examples of Joyce and Nabokov in dealing with the naturalistic descriptions of sex that were at the same time both justified and convincing.[22] He accepted an overlap between European and American writing, but identified the more personal, spontaneous, perhaps more idiosyncratic concerns he has described as an "autobiographical shapelessness" that forms the distinctive aspect of American fiction in contrast to the knowledge of a fixed social order or a defining theology that provides the English novel with a perspective unavailable to Americans. Although he resists the attempt to find in his work a source of autobiographical truth (more immediate in his short stories, he admits, than in his novels), Updike insists that abandoning that personal element exposes the writer to the risk of mechanically investing his fiction with fact at the expense of an animating intensity.[23]

Updike has perhaps provided the most forceful rebuttal to those critics who objected to his reluctance to condemn Rabbit. In an often quoted comment, he noted the "yes-but" aspect of his work, "Yes in *Rabbit, Run,* to our inner urgent whispers, but – the social fabric collapses murderously."[24] This complex view of the novel was noted by Granville Hicks, who found redeeming qualities in Rabbit and a compassionate response by Updike. For Hicks, one of many who have commented on it, the epigraph from Pascal serves as a summary of the novel in which Rabbit's "motions of Grace" are balanced against the hardness of his heart and the external circumstances which both victimize him and prompt him to delude himself about his prospects.[25] An alternative reading is proposed by Margaret Hallisy, who sees Rabbit's dilemma ironically reflected in Pascal's thought about the duality of man as both limited and omnipotent. Hallisy views Rabbit as a man of faith who feels the presence of God but who receives the diluted wisdom of Pascal from his former coach Marty Tothero. Confronted with that spiritual emptiness, Rabbit vacillates, ultimately running from the moral ambiguity in a futile attempt to substitute physical motion for his lost faith.[26]

Perhaps responding to the critical tendency to seize on relatively narrow clues as definitive expressions of a novel, Updike has protested that it is possible to overstate the importance of the epigraph which he took from an Everyman edition. He changed the translation of the French original, the phrase "the spirit of Grace" becoming "the motions of Grace," and restored the punctuation, bringing it closer to the original; thus the motions of grace and the hardness of the heart appear on one side of the semicolon and the external circumstances on the other.[27]

These external circumstances were, for Updike, everywhere Rabbit turns, from pregnancy and family responsibilities to the financial problems that press in upon him. The motions of Grace, he explained, represented our nonmaterial side that seeks out what is good, and the hardness of the heart, with which Grace is intertwined, a contrasting expression of Rabbit's character.[28] While hidden in what he thinks of as the safety of his former coach's apartment, Rabbit is directed to where "men are busy nailing the world down, and toward the disembodied sounds his heart makes in darkness a motion of love."[29]

In fact, however, Rabbit's concluding meditation on motion and his subsequent ecstatic attempt to fulfill its potential lead him in another direction. Rabbit dismisses as insubstantial the crowded field of social experience and its consequent confusions. "Funny," he thinks, "how what makes you move is so simple and the field you must move in is so crowded. Goodness lies inside, there is nothing outside, those things he was trying to balance have no weight" (308). The balance, which in the epigraph appears to be maintained by a semicolon separating the motions of Grace and the hardness of the heart from external circumstances, here seems shifted exclusively to an internal arena in which competing claims may be examined. "The way of life is wonderful; it is by abandonment," declares Emerson, in whose transcendental philosophy critics have found justification for Rabbit's actions. For Emerson, however, abandonment proceeds from the "flames and generosities of the heart," which, though it refuses to be imprisoned, prompts the circular movement that allows us to transcend the transience of things.[30] Like William Young of Updike's story "Museums & Women," Rabbit searches for a radiance that continues to fade behind him at each encounter with what come to be seen as the increasingly familiar joys of domesticity. The resistance to such contentment in Denis de Rougemont's suggestive elaboration of his mythic treatment of love in the Western world, prompts some of Updike's more strenuous reservations. Nonetheless, although he sees as finally unconvincing de Rougemont's obstructed and narcissistic view of love, he acknowledges that it accurately describes a means of self-assertion in which "The heart prefers to move against the grain of circumstance."[31]

The conflict between self-assertion and the insistent claims of the substantial world often centers in Updike's fictions around the mediating force of religion, to which, Updike has remarked, we optimistically look for a "guarantee that our self enjoys an intended relation to the outer world."[32] Acknowledging the "culture of common experience" depicted in *Rabbit, Run,* Thomas Edwards contended the novel was so distinctly an expression of the 1950s because it "takes so little account of the public terms of life in its time."[33] Similarly, noting what he termed Updike's accurate representation of the "minutiae of the Eisenhower age" – indications of class and status that ranged from the glamor of high school heroes to the authority invested in athletic coaches and included the way generational tensions both pulled at family life and looked to it as a sustaining value – Richard Locke felt that finally Rabbit operated within his inner spaces.[34]

Still, as Edward Vargo points out in calling attention to the sacralized dimensions of *Rabbit, Run,* Rabbit's failure to integrate his religious feeling with any paradigmatic myth or ritual act other than sports, sexuality, or running or, briefly, in the rite of Christian burial prevents his meaningful or sustained communion with the unseen world.[35] In contrast, Dean Doner finds the traps from which Rabbit runs – a joyless marriage, a stifling economy, and a general lack of excellence that afflicts middle-class American life – all signs of an oppressive humanism that runs throughout Updike's fiction. Doner identifies an opposition between the guilt that attends earthly considerations of happiness for which the humanist Reverend Jack Eccles is perhaps the principal spokesman, and the higher promptings Rabbit glimpses of his soul. Rabbit becomes lost, Doner points out, when he attempts to follow a road map rather than his intuitive sense of an unseen world. Accordingly, Rabbit rejects the sociological view of religious consolation offered by the comically portrayed Reverend Eccles; he inarticulately and intuitively clings to the belief in an unseen world that redeems the otherwise empty landscape.[36]

In thus reducing humanism to a middle-class materialism indifferent to the needs of the spirit and responsible for the deterioration of values that describes contemporary urban life, Doner misses the ambivalence with which Updike views it and the sustaining, even transcendent, human qualities of the ordinary urgings of sex and the institutional ceremony of church and the sacramental nature of marriage. It is, finally, Rabbit's ecstatic escape from these that leaves him directionless. His resistance to the unseen world must be validated as much as his belief in it must be celebrated.

Updike has defended Rabbit's attempt to escape the constraints on self-realization and individual freedom that marriage imposes, claiming there is a case to be made for running away from one's wife and that what he intended to show in the novel was "the shadow of moral ambiguity."[37] At the same time, he has described Rabbit as a victim of the "dreadful freedom" that comes with absorption in one's personal life, in large measure resulting from the lack of purposive vocation and the consequent boredom that has left the American middle class struggling with problems that once troubled only the aristocracy.[38]

Updike has acknowledged that though the novel "had a few overheard news items in it, it wasn't really in a conscious way about the 50's. It just was a product of the 50's."[39] The central image of running announced in the title, a movement which seems to contrast with the static self-satisfaction of the Eisenhower fifties, has over the years continued to prompt critical attention to the question of whether Rabbit is running away from or toward something, whether he represents an alternative to the mediocrity and deadness of middle-class American life in the excellence he had briefly known as a high school athlete, or is merely childlike and self-indulgent.

In their pioneering full-scale treatment, Alice and Kenneth Hamilton established the religious and moral approach much of the early criticism of Updike was to take. Viewing *Rabbit, Run* from the perspective of Kierkegaard's desire to reconcile subjective and objective truth, the Hamiltons concluded that Rabbit's search for perfection and his reliance on feelings at the expense of actuality lead him to a dead end. "The more an individual tries to know himself in isolation from his environment," they averred, "the greater becomes his capacity for self-deception and the wider becomes the gulf that separates him and his fellows and leaves him in frightening loneliness." Though they note that sexual appetites lead to a transcendent understanding, the Hamiltons suggest that the goal toward which Updike points his characters is an end to desires which exist only in the love of God and which can be approached through the sustaining vision of ceremony, notably church going.[40] That Updike finds such a limited vision of human concerns desirable is, however, questionable. More persuasive is the idea that one of the ways in which God can be approached is through the concrete experience of sexuality and that Rabbit runs as much from the polar abstractions of the Reverend Jack Eccles and the Lutheran minister Fritz Kruppenbach as from what he thinks of as the second-rate quality of middle-class life.

The difficulty of reconciling conservative religious views that seem indebted to Karl Barth's remark that "One cannot speak of God by speaking of man in a loud voice" with the moral ambiguity of Updike's fictional world has led critics such as Bernard Schopen to distinguish between the problems of morality Updike addresses in which the individual struggles against the hypocritical observance of empty social forms and those of faith, often approached through sexuality, which demand an internal or subjective integrity despite the suffering such personal fulfillment often exacts from others.[41]

In one of the more strident discussions of Updike within a religious context, Robert Detweiler finds at the center of *Rabbit, Run* a crisis described in Reinhold Niebuhr's concern with the concealment of the sinful nature of humanity along with the denial of individual responsibility. Detweiler's view of the novel as an indictment of American Protestant society thus turns on its head Updike's feeling for sensuality as a means of approaching a spiritual truth.[42] Though like Detweiler Susan Uphaus concludes that Rabbit faces a dead end, she notes that it is precisely in the ritual of sex that Rabbit comes closest to religious experience. In a suggestive discussion of the ambiguous meanings Updike associates with conventional religious images, Uphaus concludes that Rabbit's experience forcefully reveals not only the human dichotomy of physical desires and spiritual longing but a spiritual emptiness that describes contemporary society as a whole.[43]

Sex, which Updike classed with art and religion as the three great secret things, has, as the successive Rabbit novels have shown, increasingly lost much of its mystery. For Brooke Horvath, Rabbit's erotic questing perversely denies the union of sex and religion that would have allowed him to get beyond a childlike view of life as a game in which he has been designated to play a special role and the consequent dissatisfactions with the present he continues to experience. Horvath, who notes the influence of de Rougemont's *Love in the Western World* on Rabbit's avoidance of human relationships, relies heavily on the work of psychologists Rollo May and Sam Keen in attributing the hero's failed quest to his belief in the myths of American capitalism and subsequently to the counterculture's confusion of the sexual revolution which linked love with violence and death on the one hand and fulfillment on the other. The failure of nerve that Rabbit demonstrates in the first three novels, Horvath concludes, leads to his abandoning an earlier visionary vitality and ultimately to his retreat *into* adulthood.[44]

The inner and external forces that inform Rabbit's search for selfhood and his regard for family are, in Kerry Ahearn's view, made up of self-contradictory impulses that come together at the point of adultery. Examined less in terms of linear plotting than in the opposition of image-pairs, Rabbit's career is shown to reflect the archetypal American hero's ambivalent escape from women and society (and so from adult responsibility) to a nurturing nature on the one hand and the safety promised by marriage and community on the other.[45]

The imperative to run has thus been viewed alternately as reflecting the need to escape the deadening conformity of the period and as an act of moral irresponsibility, aimed particularly at the constraints of marriage and the restrictions on freedom represented generally by women. For Derek Wright, Rabbit's reaction to an over-defined world is compromised by his sacralizing of such material concerns as sports and sex; his rejection of the world's clutter remains self-consciously deliberate and so artificial. Accordingly, his attempt to maintain his freedom keeps him in an unthinking, mapless flight, toward as well as from all women. As objects through which Rabbit hopes to escape his feeling of imprisonment, women, like space, are equally blank. His bid for freedom in an undiscriminating sexuality can finally exist nowhere but within the form of the novel itself and the imaginative space it accommodates.[46]

Updike's tendency to regard women as sexually reassuring only when blankly docile constitutes as well the pessimistic burden of Mary Allen's limited study of the way women are depicted in American fiction of the sixties. Allen argues that Rabbit, like Updike, is comfortable only with women who allow themselves to be formed by the concepts of the male, who, struggling to escape the influence of a powerful and manipulative mother, feels threatened by any sign of female intelligence or independence. In employing women principally as a means of self-realization, Rabbit thus reflects something of the cultural attitudes of the time. Although he regards them at times with tenderness and even wonder, more often he adopts a condescending attitude that, Allen contends, allows Updike's fiction "under the guise of tolerant acceptance . . . insidiously [to go] about making female mediocrity and inertia seem inevitable, even lovable."[47]

Rabbit may not understand the impulse that leads him to mythologize women, but, Stacey Olster in her essay in this volume contends, the women themselves no less than Updike are aware of their situation. Locating *Rabbit, Run* within the broader context of the historical period in which it was written as well as of Updike's subsequent fiction, Olster believes that Rabbit's flawed view of women as a means by which he can escape his own mortality is undercut both by the hints of reality that continue to intrude on his imagination and by the more realistic assessment that women make. Olster finds the war between men and women paralleled by the battle women wage against each other, often disappointing Rabbit's inflated expectations. She concludes that Rabbit's attempt to use women as a means of transcendence ultimately leaves him emptier than the images of them he so desperately projects.

Not surprisingly, Rabbit's attempt to transcend the external circumstances of his life has also prompted a critical controversy over the existential questions it raises. Fred Standley sees Rabbit as a representative of the modern protagonist, the rebel-victim described by Ihab Hassan, tormented by anxieties and endlessly pursuing a dream he is unable to realize. Lacking a point of focus outside himself, Standley contends, Rabbit is thrown exclusively on sensations to determine truth and so allows himself to fall into a dehumanized condition projected in the animal imagery of the novel. Ultimately, Standley argues, this disoriented self-deception prevents Rabbit from discovering his identity and leads him instead to become ensnared in a trap of his own making.[48]

Perhaps reflecting something of the sensibility of the period of the sixties, David Galloway views Rabbit as a saint of the absurd who rebels against the spiritual shallowness and sterility of the world. For Galloway, the search for spiritual truth that Rabbit undertakes requires a necessary hardness of the heart and demands an absolute separation from society. Primarily a religious struggle, this rebellion represents an attempt to break from conventional ethics to pursue an inner vision that will invest life with meaning in the supposed absence of God.[49]

Like Galloway, Joseph Waldmeir sees Rabbit as embarked on a quest for identity. Waldmeir finds in this quest a precarious balance between the ideal and the pragmatic, a balance complicated in Updike's fiction by the introduction of the Christian church. In *Rabbit, Run,* its fulfillment is frustrated both by Updike's involvement with his characters and by the ironic distancing he adopts toward the ending. Seemingly a response to the waning of modernism, the contradiction of these elements emerges in Waldmeir's view of the heroic quest as Updike represents it, contenting itself with perception but lacking revelation and ultimately with no revelation to make.[50]

If for Waldmeir Updike's novel reveals less an absence of content than an unwillingness to resolve the conflict in favor of either a religious or a humanistic principle, for Howard Harper Rabbit's insistence on saying "no" to a fate he regards as not good enough links him to Camus' absurd man. He is led to embark on an existential quest that focuses less on the search for identity than on its self-justification.[51] Paul Borgman goes even further, ascribing to Rabbit's struggle for faith a tragic dimension. Unable to confirm the motions of Grace in his encounters with external circumstances, Borgman argues, Rabbit attempts to resist the compromises proposed in Eccles' rationalism and embraced by society. Unlike those critics who feel Rabbit is trying to escape himself, Borgman maintains that in running he is trying to escape those forces that would prevent him from finding himself.[52]

The notion of Rabbit as a heroic rebel is resisted in contrasting responses to the novel by J. A. Ward and Gerry Brenner. Ward is disappointed by the overall content of Updike's fiction which, characteristic of the *New Yorker*, explores only the modest insights yielded by the embarrassments of the middle class. Citing the pessimism of its outlook, Ward describes *Rabbit, Run* as an existentialist antinovel, that views experience as formless and so denies the possibility of a rational response to it. Accordingly, Ward finds that Rabbit obeys only the authority of his inner voice subordinating a moral sense to the idea of life as performance. In contrast, Brenner argues that Updike is fully alert to the consequences of Rabbit's determination to remain an Adamic figure of innocence, whose encounters with ineffectual male figures of authority are counterpointed by more powerful if intimidating matriarchal influences. Left vulnerable by the breakdown of traditional prescriptive values, Rabbit's increasingly regressive attempt to locate more sustaining ones takes the form of an irresponsible romantic dream, pursued without understanding and condemning him to a self-defeating alienation. His consequent reliance on instinct alone is exposed as an impoverished idea, leading not to renewal but to chaos.[53]

Extending Brenner's analysis of Updike's treatment of the return to nature, Larry Taylor views the novel as antipastoral satire, a critique of Rabbit's refusal to accept the loss of Eden. Rabbit's dogged insistence on maintaining idyllic norms and his consequent insistence on viewing himself as an innocent victim of a second-rate society, Taylor argues, are what prompt him to search for the ideal as though it were a geographical location which he can approach only by overcoming the obliqueness of others.[54] John Neary, on the other hand, rejects the idea of Rabbit as a figure of futility, insisting that Updike is essentially an affirmative writer indebted to Kierkegaard's Christian view of repetition as a redemptive act. Centering his discussion around the metaphor of marriage, Neary maintains that *Rabbit, Run* follows Rabbit's attempts to abandon the world only to have it miraculously restored to him. Neary's argument for a transcendent act returning the central figure to the substantive world of ordinary things seems to depend for its conviction on establishing its opposite terms. Rabbit's night-long drive, for example, only brings him back home, Janice's dullness allows him to refashion her into an Edenic dream image, and even the deconstructionist play of difference through which the ending overturns the generic conventions of the novel only anticipates a return to the real, an anticipation Neary finds confirmed in the subsequent novels in Rabbit's saga. Perhaps most instructive, however, is the shift at the center of this argument from the movements of the central figure to the external conditions over which he has no control but which ultimately determine his destiny.[55]

Rabbit is admittedly less influenced by events than are the Naturalistic heroes of Dreiser, Norris, or Farrell. In addition to allusion to topical events, however, a sense of the period emerges through the representation of such social and cultural phenomena as the spread of freeways, the influence of radio and TV, or the proliferation of shopping malls. In addition to the importance he attributes to the style of the novel, for example, Donald Greiner claims that Updike's return to Harry in successive decades allows him to "gauge his sense of how his own aging body and shrinking possibilities relate to the constantly changing course of the country."[56]

Noting that in the first draft of the novel Updike left spaces for news broadcasts he later filled in after confirming the accuracy of his information, Dilvio Ristoff finds in Rabbit's conservative reaction to events a "perfect representative of a typical American attitude of the Fifties." Ristoff thus sees Rabbit as a victim of postwar society whose conformist values he both represents and sporadically and ineffectually resists. In Ristoff's view, the tension of the novel emerges as a result of Rabbit's struggle to adapt to the social system at least as much as his unhappiness with it.[57]

Though Rabbit is painfully aware of the passage of time, the ongoing present underscores the illusion of youth and movement and so the urgency against whose background the awareness of loss emerges. Updike's realism is not in the tradition of Twain and Howells on the one hand or of Sinclair Lewis' satirical or Tom Wolfe's linguistically explosive cartoons on the other. It neither identifies status nor links sex with money. Nor is Updike closer to the stringent self-denials of James Gould Cozzens, who, he admits, he has always had trouble reading, or to the attitudinal sophistication of Irwin Shaw, to whose hero, Christian Darling, in "The Eighty-Yard Run," Rabbit bears some superficial resemblance. *Rabbit, Run* finds its ultimate source less in literary antecedents than in the community's interest in basketball Updike experienced while growing up in Berks County, Pennsylvania, and the phenomenon of the former athlete as it presented itself to his imagination. His initial treatment of the theme appeared in the story, "Ace in the Hole," he wrote in his senior year at Harvard. On graduation, he addressed the subject again in a poem, "Ex-Basketball Player," which the *New Yorker* published one year later.[58] The animating impulse of the novel, Updike maintained, rests in the tension between the "inner, intimate appetites and the external consolations of life," tensions of individual wants and strict social limits, he explained, for which there is no reconciliation.[59]

Updike underscores the point in his reservations about the conventional structure of plot and, in the process, illuminates the approach to realism which animates his fiction in contrast, say, to that of Henry James, whose well-known dicta that the real represents "the things we cannot possibly *not* know," and that art can only draw a circle which circumscribes the continual flow of experience, Updike's remarks obliquely parallel.[60] Plot, Updike acknowledged, has always been worrisome.

> I don't think that life falls into plots, it does not end quite the way books do. In that sense the bourgeois novel is a falsification of modern experience. So, I do believe that there are dead conventions and I've tried in my own way to shake free of them, and attended to the experiments of others. The novel *does* have conventions, after all, and when we pick up a novel, we do so partly because we think it's going to give us more of the same. We've enjoyed the old same. The artist is afflicted, I think, by not even knowing how *not* to provide more of the same. His conception of the novel also involves exciting events and everything kind of fitting together at the end, and all these things which may be attributes of a mode of writing more than of reality as it flows mysteriously around us and through history.[61]

Whether the focus of the novel is on the surface of experience or Rabbit's interior journey has thus been a continuing source of critical investigation which has frequently taken the form of questioning whether Updike's stylistic precision has preempted if not, in fact, contradicted the meaning of his fiction.[62] The prose style of the novel suggests to John Fleischauer a self-consciously ironic distance that prevents identification with the romantic sentimentality expressed by the characters and indicates the existence of a competing value system. Fleischauer finds this distance in the adjectival excess which seems at times to call attention to itself and adopts a precision separating the object described from the narrative of which it is only an element. Scenes, accordingly, become more important than action, space more important than time. In this stylized interruption of the structure of the sentence to call attention to its peripheral details Fleischauer finds a comedy of escape that establishes a pattern of contentment with partial or fragmented successes.[63]

In an essay written for this volume, Philip Stevick's illuminating taxonomy of Updike's prose style reveals an equally complex narrative pattern. Visually oriented, even painterly, suggesting a physical rather than an intellectual principle animating the characters, the narrative divides into a self-conscious, interruptive mode commonly identified as Updike's style, and a flat, uninflected speech, lacking in nuance and resonance that evokes the Pennsylvania of Updike's youth and expresses the longing and desire, the longing, above all, for desire and at the same time for safety that constitute Rabbit's deepest need. Thickly textured, Updike's present tense undermines at least as much as it celebrates the idea of self. Working to erase the reflective consciousness of the storyteller, it remains highly evocative, at once anxious and reassuring, rootless and assimilated, mysterious and ordinary.

Alternating between interior illumination and social observation while struggling against foreclosed possibilities, the fluid prose style thus seems to mirror the hopeful movement that lies at the center of the novel. Even Joyce Carol Oates, who regarded the ending of *Rabbit, Run* as bitterly ironic, concluded that the novel was characterized by "an odd 'Fifties' optimism despite the current of its remorseless plot."[64]

A contrasting approach is taken by Raymond Mazurek who argues that Updike grounds Rabbit's quest in the American ideology of self and, although he conveys a sense of the American postfifties, he fails to provide any distance from the protagonist or to develop a social analysis that would allow him to understand the period. Instead, transposing the social concerns of gender and class into a narrative of individual illness, *Rabbit, Run* reinforces the individualistic assumptions that informed the dominant cultural myths at the end of the period and so condemns Rabbit to a feeling of alienation within it.[65]

Similarly acknowledging that of all the Rabbit novels, *Rabbit, Run* is least responsive to public events, Matthew Wilson nonetheless finds Rabbit neither fully an outsider nor completely integrated in society but ultimately "the man in the middle, aware of his being in history." With the end of his basketball career, Wilson argues, Rabbit loses the sense of a public role that is restored only as his Emersonian view of the centrality of private man is displaced throughout the sequence of novels about him by the historical self-awareness that follows his recognition of aging and the provisionality of things. By the close of the tetralogy, Updike thus transforms him from the "traditional solitary male, fleeing society and women as representatives of that society, to a man integrated into society and surrounded almost comically, by women."[66]

Although *Rabbit, Run* has not been accorded the status of books which defined a generation, such as *The Green Hat, This Side of Paradise, The Catcher in the Rye,* or *V.*, it does, as Sanford Pinsker shows in his incisive essay in this volume, speak authoritatively about a postwar era disappointed with failed promises and about to tune in, turn off, drop out. Identifying in Rabbit both a longing for security and an erratic if more spiritual movement, Pinsker considers Updike's "deeply ambivalent vision" a reflection of opposed impulses of conformity and rebellion that betrayed a restlessness under the placid surface of an otherwise silent generation.

More a man in a sweat suit than in gray flannel, Rabbit is a blue-collar representative of the Eisenhower era as well as a reaction to its blandness. Updike has insisted that his fiction "about the daily doings of ordinary people has more history in it than history books."[67] Asked by his character Henry Bech in a mock interview if he wasn't determined to "sing America?" Updike paraphrased himself as saying "the American style and landscape and impetus were, by predetermination his meat."[68] Yet if no one immerses himself more thoroughly in the details of middle-class America than Updike, no one seems more uncomfortable with them than Rabbit. Updike went on to describe himself as "an apologist for the spirit of anarchy – our animal or divine margin of resistance to the social contract." The impulse seems animated by Rabbit's sense of his own difference from the deadening weariness he finds around him. "Is it just these people I'm outside," he wonders at one point, "or is it all America?" (33) Trying to understand a pseudotechnical word in a drugstore window one hot afternoon, he just about makes it out in an effort that comes "right at the pit of his life," when his attention is distracted by a fat woman buying two boxes of Kleenex. The fat lady doesn't sing but Rabbit's attempt to adjust to the demands of a joyless society is just about over. Looking at the faces unnaturally lit in the reflected light of the pavement and the store windows it appears they "wear the American expression, eyes squinting and mouths sagging open in a scowl, that makes them look as if they are about to say something menacing and cruel" (270).

Throughout the novel Updike signals the sense of entrapment as much in images as in actions, notably images of the net and the circle. Joyce Markle, for example, regards the circle as signaling Rabbit's defeat as a consequence of his inability to locate in life the clear goals he defines in basketball. For Markle, who sees the existential theme of *Rabbit, Run* contradicted by its stylistic tendency to confine moral sensibility to sense impressions, Rabbit can maintain his life-giving quality of specialness only by looking beyond the confining restraints of social responsibility and even human causes while engaged in an ill-defined search for meaning.[69]

Though it entangles Rabbit, the net also holds the promise of support. The crisscrossing highways and the condition of his apartment are both nets that seem to prevent his escape from the messy domesticity of his life. His brief return home for clean clothes reminds Rabbit that earlier he was "exhausted, heading into the center of the net, where alone there seemed a chance of rest." In this depressing time, the sky seems to him "blank and cold and he feels nothing ahead of him" (97). Yet his emptiness lightens his heart with a sense of possibility. It is a curiously ambiguous image and it occurs again when, after anxiously caring for his son and trying fitfully to sleep, he goes back to bed in the early morning. "On this net he lies down and steals the hour left before the boy comes to him, hungry and cold." When Rabbit learns he will not be held responsible for his infant daughter's death, he feels "the net of law slither from him. They just won't do it for you, they just won't take you off the hook" (288). Here the stabilizing quality of the image has something made even clearer in a passage Updike later deleted: "He wants jail: to be locked in place."[70] At the conclusion of the novel Rabbit locates the internal safety of a "pure blank space in the middle of a dense net" (308). That space almost at once is again described as nothingness. Like the listener who, nothing himself, confronts in Wallace Stevens' "Snow Man" the nothing that is not there and the nothing that is, Rabbit runs from one in pursuit of the other, filled with awe and wonder at the ordinary that at the same time threatens to constrict his movements.

Just as America may be said to have discovered or rediscovered several of its writers through European eyes, Poe and Faulkner notable among them, Europe, as Eric Kielland-Lund suggests in his essay in this volume, may be in the process of reinterpreting the myths American fiction has made universal in the reflection of our popular culture. To the European mind, Kielland-Lund argues, Rabbit's restless journeying reflects something of the provincialism and alienation associated with the vastness of the American continent, the observance of religion as a social palliative rather than in doctrinal terms, and with nostalgia for a pastoral ideal. Particularly striking, for Kielland-Lund, are the lack of civility in, and abrasive nature of, the exchanges between men and women coupled with the superficial endearments they frequently employ to mask that largely masculine aggression. Rabbit is indecisive, self-indulgent, salacious, insecure, in short something like the "little man" who, in the hands of Thurber and Benchley, emerged in the pages of the *New Yorker* as a comic prototype. Updike has contended that as a writer of the fifties his interest was in "forestalling apocalypse" in contrast to writers of the next generation who, it seemed to him, had more of an interest in bringing it on.[71] As Rabbit grew older and more prosperous, increasingly touched by the awareness of his own mortality and the role of society in softening its terrors, this conservative impulse became more pronounced. Yet it is the anarchic vein that perhaps runs most deeply in *Rabbit, Run,* surely informing the concluding exhilaration and relief with which he takes off, one more time, in what seems like an unending and joyful American determination to leave the settled arrangements of society for the imagined if desperate release of personal freedom. This impulse recalls Natty Bumppo and Huck Finn, but it informs as well a series of others ranging from Jimmy Herf and later Dean Moriarty to the Invisible Man and even more recently Chief Bromden and Benny Profane. It establishes the direction in which Rabbit, finally, is headed – not from side to side across the country or even in circles, but up, up where he is immersed in the fluid movement of reality, but insulated from and so innocent of its meaning and where its careful order lies spread out before him.

NOTES

1 I am indebted for these figures to Cathy Zuckerman at Alfred A. Knopf and to Leona Nevler at Ballantine Books (Fawcett, Crest). Editions are subject to a continuous process of minor revision as typographical errors are brought to Updike's attention.

2 John Updike, "Why Rabbit Had to Go," *New York Times Book Review* (August 5, 1990): 1, 24.

3 John Updike, "A Special Message to Subscribers," *Rabbit, Run* (Franklin Center, Pennsylvania: Franklin Library, 1977). See also "Why Rabbit Had to Go."

4 John Updike, "Interview," in *First Person: Conversations on Writers and Writing,* ed. Frank Gado (Schenectady, NY: Union College Press, 1973), p. 80.

5 Letter from John Updike to ST, May 2, 1992.

6 Ibid.

7 Stanley Edgar Hyman, "The Artist as a Young Man," *New Leader* 45 (March 19, 1962): 22–3. David Boroff, "You Cannot Really Flee," *New York Times Book Review* (November 6, 1960): 4, 43.

8 Richard Gilman, "A Distinguished Image of Precarious Life," *Commonweal* 73 (October 28, 1960): 128–9.

9 Milton Rugoff, "American Tragedy: 1960," New York *Herald Tribune Book Review* (November 6, 1960): 7.

10 John Thompson, "Other People's Affairs," *Partisan Review* 28 (January–February 1961): 120–2.

11 George Steiner, "In a Rut," *The Reporter* 23 (December 8, 1960): 81–2.

12 Whitney Balliett, "The American Expression," *New Yorker* 36 (November 5, 1960): 222–4.

13 "Desperate Weakling," *Time* 7 (November 1960): 108.

14 Unsigned review in London *Times Literary Supplement* (September 29, 1961): 648. Frank McGuinness, "In Extremis," *New Statesman* (September 15, 1961): 361. Olivia Manning, "Faces of Violence," *The Spectator* (September 15, 1961): 361.

15 Anthony Burgess, Review of *Of the Farm, Commonweal* 83 (February

11, 1966): 557–9, repr. *Critical Essays on John Updike,* ed. William Macnaughton (Boston: G. K. Hall, 1982), p. 56.

16 Albert E. Wilhelm initially called attention to these changes in "Updike's Revisions of *Rabbit, Run,*" *Notes on Modern American Literature* 5 (Summer 1981): Item 15, and subsequently in his briefer note "Rabbit Restored: A Further Note on Updike's Revisions," *Notes on Modern American Literature* 6 (Spring–Summer 1982): Item 7. For a more extensive examination of Updike's revisions, see Randall H. Waldron's "Rabbit Revised," *American Literature* 56 (March 1984): 51–67. In addition to revisions made for the Penguin edition of 1964, Waldron identifies a second revision for a reprinting of the novel by Knopf in 1970 in which the author restored to its original version some of the material he had changed in the first revision. A useful summary of the publishing history of *Rabbit, Run* may be found in Donald Greiner, *John Updike's Novels* (Athens, Ohio: Ohio University Press, 1984), n. 7, pp. 61–2. Greiner's invaluable study also examines the reception of the novel and the critical issues it has generated. Updike has mentioned his original intention for a subtitle in an interview with Charles Thomas Samuels, "The Art of Fiction XLIII:John Updike," *Paris Review* 12 (Winter 1968): 109–10.

17 Gado, pp. 92–3.

18 Gado, p. 95.

19 Samuels, 110–11.

20 For the following discussion of the conversion of Updike's novel into film I have drawn on Gary Siegel, "Rabbit Runs Down," *The Modern American Novel and the Movies,* ed. Gerald Peary and Roger Shatzkin (New York: Frederick Ungar, 1978), pp. 247–55.

21 Gado, p. 94.

22 Gado, p. 99.

23 John Updike, "Creatures of the Air" [a review of *The Bachelors* by Muriel Spark], *Assorted Prose* (New York: Alfred A. Knopf, 1965), p. 306. Updike commented on this as well in an interview with William Findlay in *Cencrastus* 15 (1984): 33.

24 Samuels, 100.

25 Granville Hicks, "A Little Good in Evil," *Saturday Review* 43 (November 5, 1960): 28. Richard Lyons ("A High E.Q.," *Minnesota Review* 1 (April 1961): 385–9), who also calls attention to the epigraph, argues that the dilemma that prompts Rabbit's flight is grounded in his own inarticulateness, the inability to communicate his mystical experience. Comparing it to the emotional intensity found in J. D. Salinger's fiction, Lyons concludes that the novel is ultimately a joyful affirmation of the conditions of life.

26 Margaret Hallisy, "Updike's *Rabbit, Run* and Pascal's *Pensées,*" *Christianity and Literature* 30 (1981): 25–32.
27 Letter from John Updike to ST, May 2, 1992.
28 Jeff Campbell, "Interview with John Updike," in *Updike's Novels: Thorns Spell a Word* (Wichita Falls, Texas: Midwestern State University Press, 1987), p. 278. A useful discussion of Pascal's thought appears in Francis X. J. Coleman, *Neither Angel Nor Beast: The Life and Work of Blaise Pascal* (New York: Routledge, 1986), pp. 202–3. Coleman points out that for Pascal the infinite is not an obstacle to belief in an incomprehensible Being known only through supernatural means but a model which affords an approach to the belief in such a Being. For Rabbit, in contrast, it is in part the vastness of existence that frightens him into flight.
29 John Updike, *Rabbit, Run* (New York: Alfred A. Knopf, 1960, rev. and rpt. 1970), p. 47. Further references will be to this edition and will appear in parentheses.
30 Ralph Waldo Emerson, "Circles," *Selections*, ed. Stephen E. Whicher (Boston: Houghton Mifflin, 1957), p. 178.
31 John Updike, "More Love in the Western World" [review of *Love Declared* by Denis de Rougemont], *Assorted Prose*, p. 299.
32 John Updike, *Self-Consciousness: Memoirs* (New York: Fawcett, Crest, 1989), p. 229.
33 Thomas R. Edwards, "Updike's Rabbit Trilogy," *Atlantic* 248 (October 1981): 94.
34 Richard Locke, review of *Rabbit Redux, New York Times Book Review* (November 14, 1981): 1–2, 12, 14, 16, 20, 22, 24.
35 Edward P. Vargo, *Rainstorms and Fire: Ritual in the Novels of John Updike* (Port Washington, N.Y.: Kennikat Press, 1973), p. 55.
36 Dean Doner, "Rabbit Angstrom's Unseen World," *New World Writing* 20 (Philadelphia: Lippincott, 1962), pp. 62–75, repr. *John Updike: A Collection of Critical Essays*, ed. David Thorburn and Howard Eiland (Englewood Cliffs, N.J.: Prentice-Hall, 1979), pp. 17–34.
37 John Updike, "A Special Message to Subscribers," *Rabbit, Run* (Franklin Center, Pennsylvania: Franklin Library, 1977). See also Eric Rhode, "John Updike Talks to Eric Rhode About the Shapes and Subjects of His Fiction," *Listener* 81 (June 19, 1969): 862–4.
38 Gado, pp. 101–2.
39 John Updike, "Why Rabbit Had to Go," 24.
40 Alice and Kenneth Hamilton, *The Elements of John Updike* (Grand Rapids, MI: William B. Eerdmans, 1970), pp. 62, 137–55.
41 Bernard A. Schopen, "Faith, Morality, and the Novels of John

Updike," *Twentieth Century Literature* 24 (Winter 1978): 523–35. Other theologically oriented examinations of the novel have ranged from George Hunt's wildly off-center focus on the Lutheran minister as the thematic center of the novel (*John Updike and the Three Great Secret Things: Sex, Religion, and Art* [Grand Rapids, MI: Eerdmans, 1980]) to Ralph C. Wood's reliance on the evangelical theology of Karl Barth to find in Updike's fiction a comic celebration of the world and the possibilities for divine redemption within it ("The Strange Moral Progress of Harry Angstrom," *The Comedy of Redemption: Christian Faith and Comic Vision in Four American Novelists* [Notre Dame, IN: University of Notre Dame Press, 1988], pp. 207–29). See also Hanspeter Dorfel, "God in John Updike's Trilogy," *Religion and Philosophy* 1 (1987): 177–96; Lewis A. Lawson, "Rabbit Angstrom as a Religious Sufferer," *Journal of the American Academy of Religion* 42 (1974): 232–46; and John Stephen Martin, "Rabbit's Faith: Grace and Transformation of the Heart," *Pacific Coast Philology* 17 (1982): 103–11.

42 Robert Detweiler, "John Updike and the Indictment of Culture-Protestantism," *Four Spiritual Crises in Mid-Century American Fiction,* University of Florida Monographs No. 14 (Gainesville, FL: University of Florida Press, 1963), pp. 11–24. Taking exception to the view of Rabbit as a hero or even an antihero of the absurd, Detweiler acknowledges Updike's interest in the ramifications of contemporary sexuality along with his expressed elegiac concern with the Protestant middle class. Though he has toned it down somewhat from an earlier version, Detweiler continues to view Rabbit as an irresponsible romantic engaged in a futile quest for an undefinable goal marked largely by his inability to resolve an oedipal dilemma. See also Robert Detweiler, "The Quest for a Vanished Grail," *John Updike,* rev. ed. (Boston: G. K. Hall, 1984), pp. 33–45.

43 Susan Uphaus, *John Updike* (New York: Frederick Ungar, 1980), pp. 19–31.

44 Brooke Horvath, "The Failure of Erotic Questing in John Updike's Rabbit Novels," *Denver Quarterly* 23 (1988): 74.

45 Kerry Ahearn, "Family and Adultery: Images and Ideas in Updike's Rabbit Novels," *Twentieth Century Literature* 34 (Spring 1988): 62–83. The struggle between a socially conventional if artificial and stifling "right way" and a more intuitive if guilt-ridden and finally unavailable "good way" is examined perceptively in Elmer F. Suderman, "The Right Way and the Good Way in *Rabbit, Run,*" *University Review* 36 (Autumn 1969): 13–21.

46 Derek Wright, "Mapless Motion: Form and Space in Updike's *Rabbit, Run,*" *Modern Fiction Studies* 37 (Spring 1991): 35–44.

47 Mary Allen, *The Necessary Blankness: Women in Major American Fiction of the Sixties* (Urbana: University of Illinois Press, 1976), pp. 121–30. Josephine Hendin (*Vulnerable People: A View of American Fiction Since 1945* [New York: Oxford University Press, 1978], pp. 88–91, 94–5) attributes the difficulty in male-female relations to the coldness of mothers, which leads the victimized males to idealize sex as a way of avoiding intimacy. As a result, males look to their wives and mistresses to free them of this oedipal influence while relying upon the woman's passivity to perpetuate their own helplessness. At the same time, Hendin acknowledges, only the pursuit of women offers the possibility of male renewal. See also Mary Gordon, "Good Boys and Dead Girls," *Good Boys and Dead Girls and Other Essays* (New York: Penguin, 1991), pp. 17–23.

48 Fred L. Standley, "*Rabbit, Run:* An Image of Life," *Midwest Quarterly* 8 (Summer 1967): 371–86.

49 David Galloway, "The Absurd Man as Saint: The Novels of John Updike," *The Absurd Hero in American Fiction* (Austin: University of Texas Press, 1966), pp. 21–50.

50 Joseph Waldmeir, "It's the Going That's Important, Not the Getting There: Rabbit's Questing Non-Quest," *Modern Fiction Studies* 20 (Spring 1974): 13–27.

51 Howard M. Harper, *Desperate Faith: a study of Bellow, Salinger, Mailer, Baldwin, and Updike* (Chapel Hill: University of North Carolina Press, 1967), pp. 165–73.

52 Paul Borgman, "The Tragic Hero of Updike's *Rabbit, Run,*" *Renascence* 29 (Winter 1977): 106–12.

53 J. A. Ward, "John Updike's Fiction," *Critique* 5 (Spring/Summer 1962): 27–41; Gerry Brenner, "*Rabbit, Run:* John Updike's Criticism of the 'Return to Nature'," *Twentieth Century Literature* 12 (April 1966): 3–14, repr. *Critical Essays on John Updike,* pp. 91–104.

54 Larry Taylor, *Pastoral and Anti-Pastoral Patterns in John Updike's Fiction* (Carbondale: Southern Illinois University Press, 1971), pp. 70–85.

55 John M. Neary, " 'Ah: Runs': Updike, Rabbit, and Repetition," *Religion and Literature* 21 (Spring 1989): 89–110.

56 Donald Greiner, *John Updike's Novels* (Athens, Ohio: Ohio University Press, 1984), p. 98.

57 Dilvio Ristoff, *Updike's America: The Presence of Contemporary American History in John Updike's Rabbit Trilogy* (New York: Lang, 1988), pp. 8–9. See also his chapter, "The Domestic Rabbit," pp. 38–74.

58 One of the first to note the importance of these early treatments, Dean Doner ("Rabbit Angstrom's Unseen World," in Thorburn and Eiland, pp. 23–4) noted that where Ace, the ex-basketball star of Updike's story, also feels the constriction of his current marital condition, his ambition is to restore the greatness he experienced in the past rather than, as is Rabbit's, to identify some state of illumination that would lift him beyond it. Others who have commented on the importance of these early versions include Alice and Kenneth Hamilton, who attribute Rabbit's dilemma in the novel to the failure of his vision rather than, as in the story, a temporary dream (*The Elements of John Updike,* pp. 137–40). Clinton Burhans finds the more stereotyped portrait of Flick Webb in the poem significantly developed in the story, whereas Kerry Ahearn ("Family and Adultery: Images and Ideas in Updike's Rabbit Novels," 64–5) contrasts the stereotyped roles of the family shown in "Ace in the Hole" with the expanded dialectic of image-pairs in the Rabbit novels. See also Updike's comments on the poem in Charlie Reilly, "A Conversation with John Updike," *Canto* 3 (August 1980): 170–1. Here Updike attributes the source of the novel to the basketball games he watched as a child when his father was a ticket-taker at the games.

59 Gado, p. 92.

60 In addition to James' essay "The Art of the Novel," the reference here is to the Prefaces to *Roderick Hudson* and *The Portrait of a Lady,* as well as an undated notebook entry in which James remarks "The *whole* of anything is never told; you can only take what groups together."

61 John Updike, "An Evening with John Updike," *Salmagundi* 57 (1982): 45.

62 Perhaps the most vehement expression of this view is that of Norman Podhoretz, whose belief that Updike has little to say and expresses that in a self-consciously exhibitionistic and mandarin style can be found in a critique that focuses largely on *The Centaur.* See "A Dissent on Updike," *Doings and Undoings: The Fifties and After in American Writing* (New York: Farrar, Straus, 1964), pp. 251–7.

63 John F. Fleischauer, "John Updike's Prose Style: Definition at the Periphery of Meaning," *Critique: studies in contemporary fiction* 30 (Summer 1989): 277–90.

64 Joyce Carol Oates, [review of *The Coup*] *New Republic* (January 6, 1979): 34–5.

65 Raymond A. Mazurek, " 'Bringing the Corners Forward': Ideology and Representation in Updike's Rabbit Trilogy," *Politics and the Muse: Studies in the Politics of Recent American Literature,* ed. Adam J. Sorkin

(Bowling Green, Ohio: Bowling Green State University Popular Press, 1989), pp. 142–60.

66 Matthew Wilson, "The Rabbit Tetralogy: From Solitude to Society to Solitude Again," *Modern Fiction Studies* 37 (Spring 1991): 6.

67 Samuels, "The Art of Fiction XLIII: John Updike," 106.

68 John Updike, "Bech Meets Me," *Picked-Up Pieces* (New York: Alfred A. Knopf, 1975), pp. 11–12.

69 Joyce Markle, *Fighters and Lovers: Theme in the Novels of John Updike* (New York: New York University Press, 1973), pp. 42–7. Perhaps the most exhaustive treatment of the circle motif in Updike's art is that of Robert Alton Regan ("Updike's Symbol of the Center," *Modern Fiction Studies* 20 [1974]: 77–96). In a densely argued essay, Regan links the circle to the Jungian mandala as a symbol of unity that Updike employs to intensify rather than eliminate Christian mystery. Circles also serve as the focus of Clinton Burhans' discussion of the structure of the novel ("Things Falling Apart: Structure and Theme in *Rabbit, Run*," *Studies in the Novel* 5 [1973]: 336–51, repr. *Critical Essays on John Updike*, ed. William R. Macnaughton [Boston: G. K. Hall, 1982], pp. 148–62). Unable to invest his rebellion against external circumstances with meaning and purpose, Rabbit, in Burhans' view, remains trapped within social institutions and the impersonal relationships they foster.

70 John Updike, *Rabbit, Run* (Greenwich, CT: Fawcett, Crest, 1960), p. 238.

71 Gado, p. 80.

2

The Full Range of Updike's Prose

PHILIP STEVICK

1

IN HIS inventive and utterly fascinating novel *U and I*, Nicholson Baker builds variations on his obsession with John Updike, his bemused envy of Updike's stature as a writer, his fascination with Updike's steady curve of success, his imagined resemblances and differences with the person of Updike, his unease with the pervasive influence of Updike in his own life and work – even though he never really discovers the kinship, the commonality of themes and temperament, that would account for such an influence. Eccentric and Shandean though Baker's narrative certainly is, it reminds a reader, nonetheless, of various interactions with a writer's work that are not eccentric at all, that are central and universal. One of these is the continuity of impression a writer's work has on the memory of a sympathetic reader. Obsessed with Updike, Baker's narrator implicitly asks, After, long after, the experience of having read Updike, what remains in the memory to account for the continuing conviction of the magnitude of his art? And Baker's answer, again and again, is not character or event, not even vision or sensibility. It is style.

"Vast dying sea": the phrase struck Baker at an early moment, he tells us, an irreducible fragment of Updike that survived his reading of him.

> In an early story a character leans his forehead against a bookcase, and considers "all the poetry he had once read evaporating in him, a vast dying sea." It's a stupendous moment in the story, in fiction, perfectly situated (at least so I remember it), but I think its stupendousness derives in part from its own plucky ability to stay afloat,

> like a lifesaving scrap of Queequeg's coffin, as the rest of the story and almost all of literature capsizes and decays in deep corrosive oceans of totalled recall.[1]

It is an imaginative motif that Baker plays again, elsewhere in *U and I,* as he does not always remember the context of a phrase precisely, does not always remember correctly the work in which it occurred, but does remember the stylistic moment, as often the only piece of flotsam to have survived an otherwise forgotten fiction.

Baker is not alone in his response. From the very start, reviewers of Updike have responded to his style. Whitney Balliett, reviewing *Rabbit, Run* in the *New Yorker* so long ago and so early in Updike's career that few readers could have known who he was and how he wrote, opens with a long, lyrical paragraph on Updike's prose. Only midway through the review does Balliett mention Harry Angstrom, small-town Pennsylvania, and the sexual crises of the novel. Clearly the milieu, the characters, the thematic tensions are all less memorable for Balliett than the vehicle, "an unceasing flow of almost invariably surprising images, which he then molds into uncluttered phrases, sentences, paragraphs, and pages that move with a sense of rhythm, timing, timbre, and volume that is impeccable."[2]

Eight years later, William Gass, reviewing *Couples,* argues over matters of structural finesse and thematic import. But it is the language that fascinates him, both for praise and derogation: Gass's essay is so heavy with small quotations that it reads like a commonplace book. An "overexertion," Gass calls these sentences: "'Her receding hollowed the dull moon. Tipped shoots searched for wider light through entropic gray. The salami he made lunch from was minced death.'"[3] In between all the reviewers and critics, there are those thousands of common readers, whose impressions and recollections of Updike are inner and private. But more than a few readers of Updike in public library copies have been startled to find, in a margin, the penciled reaction of a previous reader, a compulsive underline, an asterisk, an exclamation point: not a reaction to event or idea, but to a small piece of stylistic virtuosity.

There are two reasons why, of all the aspects of Updike's art and craft, his style should have come to have the prominence it has. One is that features of the style are foregrounded more insistently than those of any other practicing novelist. Many novelists in any time and place are clever and graceful in their way with words, but aspects of Updike's vehicle – his alterations of normal word order, for example, his esoteric (or affected) word choices, his tendency to invest a heightened, complex sensory activity in a small phrase, or his obsessive, almost metaphysical metaphors – confront the reader's attention with a rhetorical aggressiveness impossible to ignore.

The other reason is more complicated than it seems. Those traits that remain in the mind and seem to define Updike's vehicle are qualities of *one* of Updike's styles. *Rabbit, Run* is written with *two* voices, *two* epistemic grips on the world, *two* sets of rhetorical resources, played off against each other in a contrapuntal or dialogic way. Each partakes at times of the other, creating midpoints, blends of the polar extremes. Yet they remain starkly discrete. That lush, ingenious, virtuoso style is as striking as it is because it always coexists with a style whose art and craft are all in the service of what looks and sounds like a lumpish banality.

2

Janice, early in the novel, gives an account of a shopping trip in a few characteristic sentences. Heavy with alcohol and pregnancy, she reveals that, although it is still March and, pregnant, she could not possibly fit into it, she has bought a bathing suit. At once irritated and tender, Harry embraces her. She describes the suit.

> "With a strap that ties behind your neck and a pleated skirt you can take off in the water. Then my varicose veins hurt so much Mother and I went into the basement of Kroll's and had chocolate sodas. They've redone the whole luncheonette section, the counter isn't there any more. But my legs still hurt so Mother brought me home and said you could pick up the car and Nelson."[4]

Separated from its context, such dialogue is almost painful to read, so toneless is it, spoken but devoid of "voice." Quite far from being artless, it is meticulously crafted, the opening fragment, the parataxis of the third sentence, the weary lack of transition and elaboration in the last sentence, the homely words like "redone."

A little later, Rabbit walks out the front door and onto the street. Outside, the natural world contrasts with the domestic tensions within. And Updike writes a sentence of signature prose, precise and sensuous, of the kind that Nicholson Baker remembers and William Gass lingers over with misgivings.

> The Norwegian maples exhale the smell of their sticky new buds and the broad living-room windows along Wilbur Street show beyond the silver patch of a television set the warm bulbs burning in kitchens, like fires at the back of caves. (15)

Nervy and audacious, resourceful, above all evocative, it is a style like no one else's in contemporary fiction. How it is made and sustained is a difficult question to answer. But it is also difficult to remember, although essential to do so, that with this style that encompasses the sensuous and anthropomorphic Norwegian maples, the mythic recollections of caves behind the sturdy fronts of the houses on Wilbur Street, the grace and rhythm of that extraordinary sentence, is another style – that encompasses the feeling of varicose veins while shopping in a small town department store.

3

John F. Fleischauer, in his fine, perceptive study of Updike's prose style,[5] notes his pervasive tendency to elaborate the qualifying elements of a sentence so that a modifying phrase, sometimes of considerable length, interrupts the subject-verb sequence. He quotes from the 1965 story "The Bulgarian Poetess": "At one point the teacher, a shapeless old Ukrainian lady with gold canines, a *prima* of the thirties, had arisen." It is a syntactic sequence the predominance and frequency of which change somewhat during Updike's career, and its purposes seem to vary subtly. The pattern nonetheless is undoubtedly basic to the working of Updike's imagination. Less insistent in *Rabbit, Run* than in the novels of mid-career, the pattern is plentiful there, all the same. "The child, hidden – all but her ribbon – behind the back of the pew, whispers to her" (237). "This childish mystery – the mystery of 'anyplace,' prelude to the ultimate, 'Why am I me?' – ignites panic in his heart" (284). "He, who always took pride in dressing neatly, who had always been led to think he was all right to look at, blushes to feel this sincerity" (304). At times that interrupting modifier suggests the mode of attention of Updike himself – writer, draftsman, observer, lover, careful to fix the nature of the subject before allowing the verb to set it in motion. Sometimes the pattern is suggestive of an especially introspective moment in the largely superficial inner life of Rabbit. In any case, that leisurely, expansive syntactical pattern clearly belongs to the stylistic mode with which we began, the lyric, highly rhetorical, highly metaphorical style which all readers of Updike tend to think of as "Updike's style."

The polar opposite of that stylistic mode continues to startle, as one becomes used to levering it up and attending to its calculated poverty of grace and mind. Into the novel by a third, Rabbit takes a bus across town to visit the minister Eccles. "Tuesday afternoon, overcast, he takes a bus to Mt. Judge," the paragraph begins, with a subtle moment of wit surrounding the ambiguity of the reference to "overcast" (115). After that, there is not much wit. "Eccles' address is at the north end of town; he rides past his own neighborhood in safety, gets off at Spruce, and walks along. . . . He feels on an even keel. . . . They have gone bowling once and have seen four movies – *Gigi, Bell, Book, and Candle, The Inn of the Sixth Happiness,* and *The Shaggy Dog.* He saw so many snippets from *The Shaggy Dog* on the Mickey Mouse Club that he was curious to see the whole thing." What has happened here to those interrupting elements, intruding between subject and verb, could not be more obvious. The interrupting elements carry a rhythmic and cognitive valuation that has no place in a passage very closely connected to the mind of Harry Angstrom.

Or, to tap into those two stylistic modes at a different level, the three styled and stylized sentences quoted above share, besides their patterns of modification, another dimension. Each of those elegant sentences conveys an attention to the latent and the manifest, the spoken and the implicit, the evident and the mysterious, the routine and the surprising. Such a stylistic aspect is consistent and pervasive whenever the more self-conscious of the modes predominates. In the contrasting passage, the verbs make clear that no such subtlety is at work. Rabbit "takes a bus"; he "rides past," "gets off." And he "feels on an even keel."

To simplify, the two stylistic modes I have begun to describe represent, on the one hand, a voice and an imagination meant to resemble Updike himself, fully engaged, at the height of his powers and, on the other hand, a voice and an imagination meant as the quintessence of Harry and Janice and Ruth. So integrated are the two voices that a fair amount of the novel partakes of both, without in any way diminishing the authority of either.

4

Of the defining traits of Updike, the qualities that seem recurrent in the commentary of others and the aspects in his own work that he speaks of, two seem pertinent to the curious duality of style in *Rabbit, Run.* One is his special affinity for the milieu of his youth. The other is the absence of a satiric strain. In his first published interview, in *The Paris Review,* the interviewer asks about Updike's willingness to return, so many times, to the same locale – Olinger in the early stories, Mt. Judge in *Rabbit, Run,* versions of Shillington, Pennsylvania.[6] He writes of that area, Updike replies, because that is what he knows. Any number of other writers, Joyce with Dublin, Hemingway with the Michigan woods, have worked a comparable vein for similar reasons. The interviewer, unsatisfied, presses further. And Updike elaborates on the way in which that milieu impressed upon him a sense of both the coherence and the terrible limitations of experience at large. The interview moves on. But one feels that the interviewer is still unsatisfied, as the reader is likely to be. The exchange has not really caught and defined the tone of Updike's response to that remembered and recreated past: Words like acceptance and affection come easily to mind. Looking back, Updike seems to have no scores to settle, no unresolved issues, no residue of resentment.

Twain, recalling the River, and Hemingway the woods impart an Edenic quality that seems plausible and plausibly American. Embracing and accepting the village is a different matter. Here

Sherwood Anderson sets the tone, along with a handful of largely forgotten writers before him and a multitude of writers since, Sinclair Lewis, H. L. Mencken, John O'Hara, for example, virtually anyone who has touched the subject: What virtues the American small town displays are sustained in the face of repression, coarseness, bigotry, and ignorance. It is hard to think of another writer of the American twentieth century who responds to a recollection of small town origins with such lovingly detailed acceptance as Updike. If there were ever any doubt about this quality in Updike's sensibility, the first section of *Self-Consciousness,* written twenty years after the interview, would settle the matter. It is an account of a return to Shillington, comparable in its tender evocativeness to Agee's recollection of the Knoxville of his childhood but like almost nothing else.

The *Paris Review* interviewer turns to an unappealing character in *The Poorhouse Fair.* And Updike responds by disavowing any satiric intent, not only there but elsewhere. "I'm not conscious of any piece of fiction of mine which has even the slightest taint of satirical attempt. You can't be satirical at the expense of fictional characters, because they're your creatures. You must only love them, and I think that once I'd set Conner in motion I did to the best of my ability try to love him and let his mind and heart beat" (108).

Thus, to render a place Updike has carried with him all his life, and to render a cast of characters toward whom, for all their small town limitations, Updike feels no superiority, no impulse to portray them as objects of ridicule, he has crafted one kind of prose carrying traces of Harvard, the Ruskin School of Drawing, New York and the *New Yorker,* and Ipswich, Massachusetts, and another kind of prose which is a recreation of the indigenous language of the place itself. It is a species of bilingualism. And the sociolinguistics of the subject is not without its pertinence.

Bilingualism, write Halliday, McIntosh, and Strevens,[7] is, in its most obvious form, the use, by members of a language community, of a second language, with varying degrees of success, on varying occasions. Speakers of a second language, they point out, can become extremely facile; the great literary examples are Conrad and Nabokov. But "it is clear that for the great majority of bilingual speakers the L2 [the nonnative language] never replaces the L1 [the native language] as a way of living; nor is it intended to do so." The authors extend the discussion to dialect, exploring situations in which a speaker of a native dialect often masters a second dialect, which he ordinarily speaks "with an accent." And they extend the discussion to "register," or the functional levels of language use: A given speaker, say, ordinarily uses a domestic, utilitarian, middle-class set of linguistic resources but shifts, when the occasion demands, to a totally different set of resources, in a professional setting, perhaps, or at a sporting event. Just as the linguists play over the infinite permutations of the bilingual phenomenon, in *Rabbit, Run* Updike obviously recalls the shared linguistic community of his youth, its own peculiar "register," and reproduces a facsimile of it as the vehicle for substantial portions of the novel, without much distance and wholly without scorn.

"She goes into the kitchen," Updike writes of Janice in a moment of narration (254). No one is speaking. There are no quote marks. Such "voice" as the passage has is the voice of the narrator (although the passage does begin to move into something resembling indirect discourse). "She goes into the kitchen and makes another drink, stronger than the first, thinking that after all it's about time she had a little fun. She hadn't had a moment to herself since she came back from the hospital." The accent of the passage, even though one cannot hear it, is Berks County, Pennsylvania. The register is lower-middle-class house talk, flat, conventional, and without nuance. The author does not speak it any more but he can readopt it at will and reproduces it without imagining it to be foolish and without imagining that anyone else will either.

5

That flat style is highly patterned. It would have to be, made, as it is, out of the conventionalities of a middle-range, unreflective experience in which habits and formulas of mind and language are essential. But it is the more dense and self-conscious modality that readers and critics refer to when they note, as they always do, that Updike's style is noticeably patterned and repetitive.

Elizabeth Tallent is wonderfully observant on the subject.

> In *Rabbit, Run,* even language itself seems secretly anxious, as if confronting some fear it can neither precisely counter nor entirely evade. There is an almost placatory reliance on certain words – placatory in the sense that any rhythm is, at some level, an attempt to stave off uncertainty, to fortify oneself against those things in the world that are frighteningly arbitrary. . . . The key words are smooth as mantras, narrow sounds snapped free of context, pure objects of contemplation, the stones that Rabbit touches again and again in his nervous circling.[8]

Early in the novel, she observes, such words as "trap" and "net" begin to establish a pattern, their repetition echoing Rabbit's situation. Further into the novel, "things are described as 'tipped' or 'tipping,' until the entire physical universe seems precariously out-of-balance." And throughout the novel, from its title to its last word, variations on the word "run" center the action of the novel, giving it its own special drive and energy.

Elizabeth Tallent is by now not alone in observing the iterative usage of a small group of words that seem intended to define Rabbit's situation, not only "trap" and "net" but "web" and "cave" and "box." And she is not alone in suggesting an incantatory, quasi-religious effect. "Ceremonial," Richard H. Rupp calls the style, describing some of the same features identified by Tallent.[9] Perhaps also obvious although not so much remarked is a whole class of what look like merely descriptive words – "house," "walls," "windows," "shades" – repeated so that they, too, define aspects of the entrapment or engulfment that the novel obsessively renders. It is no accident that a significant portion of the novel happens on the road and that the words for steering wheel and accelerator, road signs and receding highway take on a similarly iterative rhythm. Keys are lost, found, inserted, doors opened, not because the action of the novel demands it but because the very texture of the style must enact being inside and being out.

Those two elements, the arrangement of the prose so as to give a particular prominence and force to individual words and the tendency to repetition, do not, in themselves, suggest the incantatory. Richard Bridgman has traced precisely those two features as characteristic aspects of American colloquial style from mid-nineteenth century to the present time. Twain is his favorite example but he finds instances from the eighteen-twenties to Hemingway – the foregrounded word, sometimes eccentrically chosen, sometimes startlingly dialectal, the very coherence of the prose carried by its repeated elements.[10] Clearly Updike perpetuates the tradition. Yet his sensibility is so pervaded by an insistent spiritual dimension that one hears in those patterns the accents of totem and taboo and incantation.

The areas of prose at the banal extremity from the dominant elegance are patterned because the resources out of which they are made are limited and therefore predictable. Resonance of any kind is drained away and the repetitions carry no sense of chant or prayer, hardly any sense, for that matter, of urgency or complexity. Rabbit and Janice and Ruth "love" this and "hate" that, with a numbing poverty of discrimination. Something responded to positively is "great" or "nifty" or "the damndest thing." Objects of dislike are "awful," "terrible," "lousy."

Still, such patterns of repetition, both the resonant and the flat, have this much in common: a consistent and pervasive expression of desire, only occasionally fulfilled, mostly held in an unresolved suspension. The language of the novel is expressive of this longing.

At the beginning of the novel, Rabbit, playing vacant-lot basketball with a group of boys, remembers the pleasures of high school. "That his touch still lives in his hands elates him. He feels liberated from long gloom" (6). At the end of the novel, "with an effortless gathering out of a kind of sweet panic," he runs (309). Between the two, he "keeps hoping"; "expects to learn"; he "cares"; he "tries"; he "is being drawn"; he "waits"; he "wants." Above all, he is afraid, again and again, often with the frailest of justification or no justification at all. Not for nothing is his last name Angstrom. "Rabbit doesn't want to tell him anything. The more he tells, the more he loses. He's safe inside his skin, he doesn't want to come out" (125). To speak of pattern and repetition in Updike's prose style is to speak of the ways in which some very central and highly charged modes of being in the world are described and suggested and enacted in the verbal texture of the work.

6

In more ways than these, however, *Rabbit, Run* coheres through the patterns of its prose. One way is its virtuoso attempt to catch the experience of the eye, the whole visual sensorium, in the language of the book. Updike's early interest in the visual arts is widely known to his readers, as is his extraordinary work, in his maturity, as an art critic. It would be obvious, even to a reader who did not know these things, that the imagination of *Rabbit, Run* is relentlessly and ingeniously visual. It is not only visual in the sense that allows us to speak of certain writers as "impressionists," the prose being designed to catch, like an impressionist canvas, the phenomenology of sight. It is quite basically and literally eye-centered.

> She was shy about him seeing her. She made him keep his eyes shut. (11)
>
> There are so many red lines and blue lines, long names, little towns, squares and circles and stars. He moves his eyes north. (36)
>
> Tothero just stands there holding on and looking at him, smiling crookedly, the nose bent, one eye wide open, and the other heavy-lidded. (42)
>
> He moves his lips into one eye socket, gently, trying to say this night has no urgency in it, trying to listen through his lips to the timid pulse beating in the bulge of her lid. With a careful impartiality he fears she will find comic, he kisses also her other eye. (79)
>
> As she adjusts her face to his height her eyes enlarge, displaying more of the vividly clear whites to which her moss-colored irises are buttoned. (116)

Obviously, what is at issue in the style is not only the imagery of vision but the experience of seeing: looking, being watched, attending to, pretending not to see, controlling the effect of one's own eyes, reading the effect of the other's, responding to the eyes as erotic objects.

This kind of visual imagery not only registers color and form, light and dark; it registers modes of attention, the maintenance of "face," the heavy charge of ego valuation that often accompanies looking, the sense of kinship or distance in the thing seen, the longing for approval in the eyes of the other. Quite apart from its psychic resonance, however, the visual orientation of Updike's style is startling and unusual.

On Memorial Day afternoon, Rabbit and Ruth swim in the public pool (143). Rather she swims, he watches – her grace, her slight flirtations with danger, her erotic allure. Watching her in the pool in front of him, he imagines himself being watched by high school girls behind him. As she climbs out of the pool and settles beside him, the rhythm of the passage slows, accumulating sensory detail. And the range of its visual images runs something like this. There are those images that are painterly, in an explicit and quite directed way: "Her face, seen so close, is built of great flats of skin pressed clean of color by the sun, except for a burnish of yellow that adds to their size mineral weight." There are those images in which angle and perspective are everything: "He scrambles back to their blanket and lies down so that when she comes over he can see her standing above him as big as the sky." There is a plentiful amount of synaesthesia: "The air sparkles with the scent of chlorine." There are passages that enact the art of photography, with small details, not really noticeable in experience, clarified and fixed by the camera's eye: "She tears off her cap and shakes out her hair and bends over for the towel. Water on her back flows upwards down soft valleys of fat." And there are those acts of ordinary observation that are rendered intelligible by comparison to watching television: "Her bottom of its own buoyance floats up and breaks the surface – nothing much, just a round black island glistening there, a clear image suddenly in the water wavering like a blooey television set." All writers of fiction render the look of things and in the process develop characteristic ways of describing that serve to give the prose a measure of coherence and consistency. It is hard to think of another writer, however, who builds into the visual experience of narrative the full range of visual modalities, from something like the eye of the analytical cubist to something like the eye of the passive but transfixed watcher of television.

7

Updike's grounding of the visual imagery in the quite literal and explicit eyes of the characters suggests a larger principle. Almost everything seen, felt, and thought in *Rabbit, Run* has its origin or its parallel or its symbolic resonance in the bodies of the characters. Few novels are so relentlessly physical in their verbal texture. For a subculture – Protestant, modest, bourgeois, small town – in which personal distance tends to be scrupulously maintained and people do not touch each other very much, people do, on the contrary, touch quite a bit in *Rabbit, Run*. Those moments of physicality that are acted out and made explicit are not, however, most central to the designs of the style. Rather, the persistent and obsessive reference to the body, as if everything that is done and said by the characters originates not really in the cerebral cortex, in some locus of conscious, verbal intentionality, but instead issues from some bone or joint, some flexed and anxious muscle, some nameless pain or stress, some fold, some inner recess.

> Nelson's laughter spills from his head. (156)
>
> He makes a mouth that works up saliva and swallows it. (158)
>
> Joyce stares and hugs the wall with her shoulder blades. Her long golden stomach protrudes thoughtfully. (210)
>
> She discovers herself making lunch. (260)
>
> He took the ball of her shoulder in his hand and turned her roughly. (47)
>
> He is unconscious of their skins, it is her heart he wants to grind into his own. (76)
>
> The liverish skin under her eyes lifts and the corners of her mouth pull down in an appraising scowl. (153)
>
> This stuns her skin in a curious way, makes it contract so that her body feels squeezed and sickened inside it. (186)

Elevating examples such as these, taken out of their context, make *Rabbit, Run* seem more eerie than it is, as if the characters were automata perhaps, or merely the sum of their anatomies. Readers don't feel that way about the human figures in Updike's novel, as they read. Still, those passages do exist, with many more like them, with aspects or portions of the body foregrounded, as initiators, or recipients, of an action. It is a stylistic emphasis so odd and so insistent that it seems a special intent of Updike's.

By now the idea of nonverbal communication or "body language" is so familiar that it is thoroughly assimilated: One notes features of body language as part of the texture of our dailiness, no more or less remarkable than noting the clothing, the weather, or the local newspaper, within the perimeter of our observable experience. It is easy to forget how recent a deliberate, systematic observation of body language really is. Chance observations on the subject extend back to antiquity and novelists such as Sterne and Dickens integrated into their fictions their obvious fascination with stance and gesture, distance and posture, a highly charged consciousness of one's own body and the bodies of other people. In the late fifties, however, figures such as Ray Birdwhistell began fashioning an ingenious mixture of anthropology, linguistics, even art history, into something called "kinesics." Weldon Kees and Jurgen Ruesch published *Nonverbal Communication,* a wonderfully incisive set of lay observations, in 1956. At the end of the fifties, Erving Goffman began his eccentric but essential series of publications on social microbehavior. Bibliographies on gesture and nonverbal communication reveal an explosion of interest in the early sixties. And people alive and reading then can remember the ubiquitous paperbacks purporting to tell a mass audience how to "read" other people's body language.

There is something of that new awareness in Updike, no doubt an interest in bringing to his method the heightened concern with nonverbal language that had become so fascinating to the general culture. Some of that imagery of the body is expressive and semiotic and some of it is not; sometimes Updike seems to be finding his own way of rendering "body language" and sometimes he seems to be interested, rather, in the infinite variety of human shapes and sizes, the irreducible there-ness of our physicality.

Rather than drawing on an idea outside of Updike's fiction, it does seem more profitable to infer an implicit inner principle. At first sight, all that unites that extraordinary range of situations in which physicality figures in the local details of the style is a quality of oddness, eccentricity, perhaps a willed perversity, a quality that suggests that the writer and his narrator are caught slightly by surprise, as if no amount of observation could prepare one for the next nose, the next ears, the next stance and carriage. "He makes a mouth that works up saliva and swallows it as he leaves the stucco house" (158). "Mrs. Angstrom has four-cornered nostrils. Lozenge-shape, they are set in a nose that is not so much large as extra-anatomical; the little pieces of muscle and bone are individually emphatic and divide the skin into many facets in the sharp light" (159).

Second, what unites many, not all, of those passages that concern the body is that they focus on aspects of physicality that are unconscious. The deliberate stance, the purposeful gesture, the face consciously composed, none of these interests Updike very much. What does interest him is saliva and the planes of the nose. "He thins his lips over his slipping teeth like a man with stomach trouble biting back gas. He is being nibbled from within" (162). "Ruth's face across from him takes some of the pale glare of the table-top, the skin of her broad forehead shines and the two blemishes beside her nose are like spots something spilled has left" (95).

Third, a common tone unites the descriptions of the physical. *Rabbit, Run* is a novel full of victims. Except for a few functionaries and walk-on figures, everyone in the novel is a victim. What they are victims of is complex, fluid, amorphous, and not at all specific. But one thing clearly victimizes everyone in the novel: their own palpable bodies, betraying at every point, as they do, the characters' sense of self, undercutting their sense of their own wholeness and dignity and sexual allure, diminishing their claims to some importance in their world. "Pathos" is perhaps the right word for such a tone. Eccles "stands edgily, with his chest faintly cupped. He has long reddish eyebrows that push a worried wrinkle around above the bridge of his nose, and a little pale pointed knob of a chin tucked under his mouth" (102). Poor Eccles. Wishing to be a person of substance, he is diminished by his chin and the bridge of his nose. Poor Rabbit. Poor Janice. Poor Ruth. Poor all of us, for whom the idea of the self is never sufficiently complemented by the bones and the skin, the wrinkles and the curves. And so it is that a sense of the body is, in *Rabbit, Run,* not an idea, or a thematic concern, or a continuing set of motifs; it is an intimate aspect of the verbal texture of the fiction, an aspect of its prose style, like nouns and verbs.

8

Verbs? Is it possible to have gone this far and written this much without mentioning the most striking aspect of the prose of *Rabbit, Run?* Its normative tense is the present, not the past. If nothing else marks Updike's novel as a remarkable tour de force, his choice of tense would do so. It is not only possible to seem to avoid the issue in the present essay; it is possible to read considerable amounts of criticism, from the earliest reviews to the most leisured and considered commentary, without finding the question of the novel's tense really dealt with.

It is, or was, on Updike's mind. In two early interviews, he speaks of it. In one of them, the interviewer raises the question of the conscious use of cinematic technique in *Rabbit, Run,* and its use of the present tense. Updike replies:

> It was conceived of as a movie. Originally, I had a short introductory section in italics talking about entering a theater; having entered the theater, the reader was presumably sitting down and watching the opening in which the kids are tossing the basketball around while the super-imposed title and credits rolled. And my use of the present tense was in some way to correspond to the continuous present of a movie.[11]

In the other conversation, the interviewer turns to the relationship between novel and film in contemporary culture. Might a novelist now feel at a disadvantage because of the "instantaneousness and completeness of the image" in film? Yes indeed, Updike responds, musing over the convention of the novel as history, cast in the past tense, with a presiding, Godlike novelist, as in nineteenth-century novels, or without one, as in novels now. *Couples,* he says, is an old-fashioned novel, in the past tense, even dealing out conclusions for all the major characters in the last chapter.

> In *Rabbit, Run* I liked writing in the present tense. You can move between minds, between thoughts and objects and events with a curious ease not available to the past tense. I'm not sure it's as clear to the reader as it is to the person writing, but there are kinds of

> poetry, kinds of music you can strike off in the present tense. I don't know why I've not done a full-length novel in it again.[12]

As is often the case with remarks in an interview, there is the pleasure of the transcribed voice of the author himself, countered by the fact that the observations don't really take us very far. For *Rabbit, Run* the author explained the original cinematic intent, the idea of the continuous present, and the potential fluidity of movement in the rhythm of the narrative. Surely more is at stake in the choice of tense.

Of the critics, Donald Greiner observes that the present that encompasses the action of *Rabbit, Run* is Updike's present as he wrote the text, the events and the artifacts of Rabbit's ambient culture being those of the author.[13] More precisely and incisively than anyone else, John Neary expands on other dimensions of immediacy implicit in the text, first noting the sheer uncommonness of Updike's tour de force (including, at length, the sequels to *Rabbit, Run*).

> I know of no literary work of a thousand pages or more than the Rabbit series that employs the present-tense form throughout. (*Gravity's Rainbow*, at nearly nine-hundred present-tense pages, comes close – which startlingly suggests that Updike and Pynchon are literary kin.)[14]

It is certainly true: the immediacy, the fluidity, the cinematic cutting. But what finally seems more remarkable in Updike's use of the present tense is what is quite purposely and calculatedly lost. What is lost is a sense of memory, or virtual memory, implicit in the narration of the novel.

Narratives are told as if they were remembered. An autobiographical novel may very well be made of elements many of which are, in fact, remembered. But even novels that are in no way autobiographical are told with a deliberate, retrospective distance, with an illusion of recollection. History retains the illusion of personal recollection, although it is rarely possible that the historian's memory of the events related plays a significant role. Implicitly, every novel "sees" as it does, values as it does, takes the shape that it does because its writer imagines it to be the product of a plausible memory. Take any sentence from any novel and calculate the levels of pastness implicit in it as an act of virtual memory. "Under certain circumstances there are few hours in life more agreeable than the hour dedicated to the ceremony known as afternoon tea." It is the first sentence of *The Portrait of a Lady* and it implies a long experience, a ripe maturity, a willingness to discriminate among remembered occasions; mostly it sets a frame, heavy with the illusion of personal memory, within which a particular story, set in the past and apparently recollected, is about to be told.

Turn again to the tenses of *Rabbit, Run:* "She discovers herself making lunch" "The telephone rings again" "Janice replaces the receiver" "Rebecca screams" (260–3). I quote from the most painful scene in the book but it hardly matters. The effect is the same elsewhere. Without a retrospective narration, without the interposition of a period of time between the events and the telling of them, without the appearance of a mediating consciousness and a strenuous memory, the events seem slightly dislocated and decontextualized, the characters more than a little fragile and vulnerable. Every thematic commentary on *Rabbit, Run* remarks on the rootlessness and alienation that leave all the characters devoid of passion or resolve or even a stable sense of self. What such commentaries do not remark is that the style of the novel, with its insistent present tense and its illusion of not having issued from a deliberate, recollecting mind, is an extraordinarily potent technique for dramatizing the terrible loneliness of those figures.

9

If the style of Updike has been widely praised, it has also been widely derogated. It is time to face the nature of the derogation and measure its justness. Often witty at Updike's expense, the negative opinions offer variations on a single theme. The theme is this: Too clever by half, Updike's style is virtuosity for its own sake. Self-indulgent and narcissistic, it draws attention to its own ingenuity rather than serving the integrated ends of the fiction in which it appears. The more deliberate criticism that has addressed Updike's work in recent years has tended to avoid the epigrammatic cut that came so easily to earlier reviewers and essayists;

rather, insofar as it finds Updike's style problematic, it has cast the matter, again and again, in diagrammatic terms. The style is of the outside and the question is what, if anything, is inside.

From the start, commentators on Updike's work have used the word "surprise" or one like it to describe the effect of his use of language. Sometimes, surely, the word is used as a tribute to his virtuosity, like a tribute one might give a successful trapeze act. But just as surely, noting the surprising quality of the style is sometimes meant to remark on Updike's apparent intent to impose a design on the reader, to leave him changed in small but substantive ways. Insofar as that design is intended, and successful, it suggests that the style, even at its most foregrounded, is never its own end, but always kinetic, highly charged, intended to direct a reader toward some dense, anxious, and problematic center.

Near the middle of the novel, Rabbit runs, this time to the maternity waiting room of the hospital. The imagery, as he runs, is of store fronts, moving past the eye, with something of the rhythm of the runner's consciousness. "Insurance agencies with photographs of tornado damage in the windows." Railroad tracks "slide between walls of blackened stone soft like moss through the center of the city" (194). It is a descriptive touch just eccentric enough to draw attention to itself, surprising, as if the railroad tracks were the source of their own energy and direction, were able to slide between buildings. A slight suggestion of the erotic might seem a quality evoked in the reader's eye in anybody else but not in Updike, where almost everything is eroticized sooner or later, even railroad tracks. It is a grim, dark, decaying city; but the railroad tracks ingratiate their way into it. The neon lights of the dives along Railway Street impart "sunset tints of pink" to tracks which now lie below, in a hollow. "Music rises to him. The heavy boards of the old bridge, waxed black with locomotive smoke, rumble under his feet. Being a small-town boy, he always has a fear of being knifed in a city slum."

One aspect of the passage that claims the reader's attention is its abrupt variety, moving, as it does, from bare, quick description ("darkened candy stores") to moments of sensuous lyricism ("threads of metal deep below in a darkness like a river") to momentary insights into Harry's consciousness ("Being a small-town boy"), an abrupt variety, as well, of tone, the soft and familiar together with the dark and sinister. What else surprises is that gracefully intrusive railroad track and the idea of music rising from footfalls on a wooden bridge, the self-generated sound dispelling the fears of the dark and deserted cityscape. The passage seems anything but conventional; it seems quite self-consciously styled. Yet nothing seems precious or overdone, clever for its own sake. And everything seeks, slightly but unmistakably, to leave the reader in a different place from the one where he expected to be.

Every sentence in the passage I cite and half the sentences elsewhere in the book represent a small response to a consistent thematic concern of *Rabbit, Run,* implicit in the first scene, implicit in the last: a thematic concern that could be called, at the risk of banality, the comforts of home. There is never any doubt that it gives Updike great pleasure to evoke the places of his childhood; and it gives Rabbit great assurance to be there, among the street names and the television programs that surround him with a cushion of familiarity. It is also a terrible place to be, small and small minded, turned in on itself, a maze without an exit, a trap, a cul de sac. It is also everything in between, every midpoint and permutation. Rabbit never articulates this endless ambivalence and there is no narrative voice to do so. It is the function of the prose style to register the multitude of ways, many of them quite startling and unexpected, in which the characters of *Rabbit, Run* feel variously comfortable, assimilated, at home, or, on the other hand, anxious, rootless, and disconnected.

The prose seeks to alter our modes of attention. The ordinary becomes vexed and extraordinary; responding, the reader is drawn into the problematics of the novel. The customary and routine becomes sensuous and remarkable. The sacred becomes profane and the profane sacred. The literal becomes lyrical. And ordinary names for ordinary things prove insufficient to signify their ineffable mystery.

In the maternity ward, about to see his baby, Rabbit follows a nurse, assessing her as a sexual object; the style is that flat and banal mode that seems most directly to express Rabbit's mind: she looks like "a good solid piece." He carries with him the pathos of a guest on a television program whose domestic heartbreak he has been watching in the lounge, "a woman from Springfield, Illinois." Imagining, for a moment, that those two touches are meant to render Rabbit as appallingly callow, the reader might conclude, at a second glance, that they honor him. The style, in some uncanny way, permits both. The words are chosen to evoke a robust quality, quite without guile. Arranged in a row, the newborn babies' heads look, to Rabbit's eye, like oranges in a supermarket. Yet a sentence or two later, he responds to the planes and wrinkles of his baby's face with such attention and tenderness that the moment is transformed into an experience more sacred than all the ostensibly religious moments in the novel.

A case can always be made that the style is self-indulgent. But a reader who wishes to maintain that the stylistic effects are ornamental would do well to note the tendency of the prose to destabilize its audience, drawing it into the center of its troubling and ambivalent vision.

NOTES

1 *U and I: A True Story* (New York: Random House, 1991), p. 33.
2 "The American Expression," *New Yorker* 36 (Nov. 5, 1960): 222–4.
3 "Cock-a-doodle-doo," in *Fiction and the Figures of Life* (New York: Knopf, 1970), pp. 209–10.
4 *Rabbit, Run* (New York: Alfred A. Knopf, 1960; rev. and rpt. 1970), p. 12. Subsequent references, which appear parenthetically in the text, are to the 1970 edition.
5 "John Updike's Prose Style: Definition at the Periphery of Meaning," *Critique* 30 (Summer 1989): 277–89.
6 Charles Thomas Samuels, "The Art of Fiction XLIII: John Updike," *Paris Review* 12 (Winter, 1968): 85–117.
7 M. A. K. Halliday, Angus McIntosh, and Peter Strevens, "The Users and Uses of Language," in *Readings in the Sociology of Language*, ed. Joshua A. Fishman (Mouton: The Hague, 1970).
8 *Married Men and Magic Tricks: John Updike's Erotic Heroes* (New York: Creative Arts, 1982), pp. 78–9.
9 *Celebration in Postwar American Fiction 1945–1967* (Miami: University of Miami Press, 1970).
10 *The Colloquial Style in America* (New York: Oxford University Press, 1966).

11 *First Person: Conversations on Writers and Writing*, ed. Frank Gado (Schenectady: Union College Press, 1973), p. 95.

12 Samuels, 111.

13 Donald J. Greiner, *John Updike's Novels* (Athens: Ohio University Press, 1984), p. 49.

14 *Something and Nothingness: The Fiction of John Updike and John Fowles* (Carbondale: Southern Illinois University Press, 1992), p. 46.

3

Restlessness in the 1950s: What Made Rabbit Run?

SANFORD PINSKER

These are the tranquilized *Fifties*.

–Robert Lowell, *Life Studies*

MUCH of Robert Lowell's "Memories of West Street and Lepke" is unabashedly personal, a ruthless raiding of private experience that overturns formalistic assumptions about aesthetic distance and replaces them with a plainspoken "I," clearly and undeniably the voice of the poet himself. Other dark, latter-day Romantics such as Sylvia Plath, Anne Sexton, and W. D. Snodgrass soon followed in a bursting forth of what came to be known as "confessional poetry," but it was Lowell's *Life Studies* (1959) that made the new candor possible. No longer was poetry, as in T. S. Eliot's formulation, "an escape from personality," but rather a wallowing in the private, often humiliating, details of one's private life – without the knotty, metaphysical language that characterized Lowell's earlier poetry (for example, "The Quaker Graveyard in Nantucket") and certainly without the obligation to speak the unspeakable through a dramatic mask.

I begin with Lowell's characterization of the fifties as a way to test out just how anxious, how jumpy, the age of conformity actually was; and how much rebelliousness the decade generated. Later, I'll suggest the ways in which *Rabbit, Run* – published in the same year as *Life Studies* – employs formalist techniques (the very ones Lowell abandoned) to give this ambivalent decade an objective correlative and a human face.[1] That said, I start with the obvious: The "tranquilized *Fifties*" is one of those phrases that rings with authority and sticking power. No matter that it revealed more about Lowell than about the popular culture or that he was at best only slightly aware of the world according to *Time* or *Life*. Poetry alone mattered to him because only poetry existed in a realm where busy executives and the daily newspapers would never want to tamper. Nonetheless, Lowell was dead right about the restlessness and insecurity that drove an astonishing number of people to Miltown, the 1950s tranquilizer of choice: If the face the 1950s projected to the world seemed placid, tranquilizers had something to do with it. In this sense, Lowell's phrase was a savvy pun on those jittery, uncertain times.[2]

Nor was Lowell alone in sensing a dark underside to the decade's "proper and prim" public face of tidy suburban lawns and Madison Avenue ads. Others also noticed the ticks of regret, the signs of incipient rebellion, just beneath the folds of gray flannel suiting. *Rabbit, Run* is the portrait of a would-be rebel's rise and fall, the story of an ordinary man's extraordinary effort to break out of the domestic trap as the 1950s defined it. That Rabbit racks up a certain number of human casualties in his ill-defined flight is true enough; that his isolated moments of "running" prove exhilarating is compelling. What Updike adds are considerations of how rebellions *fail*, how consequences mount and guilts accumulate.

As Irving Howe puts it in a seminal 1954 essay entitled "The Age of Conformity": "To what does one conform? To institutions, obviously. . . . [However] what one conforms to most of all – despite and against one's intentions – is the zeitgeist, that vast insidious sum of pressures and fashions. . . . Only, some resist and some don't."[3] Howe's essay is an attack on those – principally, Lionel Trilling – who had too easily accommodated themselves to postwar affluence; and a reminder that there was still a place, and a need, for radical dissent. Of the intellectuals who responded to *Commentary* magazine's 1952 symposium on "Our Country and Our Culture," Howe and Norman Mailer alone represented positions that Trilling later defined, and largely dismissed, as the dreary, predictable stuff of an adversarial stance. A few years later Howe, Mailer, and others launched an intellectual quarterly whose title said it all: *Dissent.*

Meanwhile, the mainstream of the 1950s muddled on, barely paying attention to squabbles that seem to matter far more to New York intellectuals than to folks buying their first lawnmower and television set. Cultural historians tend to evoke the years between 1945 and 1960 through a series of quick snapshots, visual symbols of what America was, and what it became, during the years that followed World War II: "I Like Ike" campaign buttons; Levittown, the nation's first suburban housing tract; the House Un-American Activities Committee; the Hollywood Ten; Senator Joseph McCarthy; Alger Hiss; the Rosenbergs. With the possible exception of Eisenhower, each item on this list generated a fair amount of controversy in its time, and some – for example, Julius and Ethel Rosenberg, the spies accused of providing vital information about the atomic bomb to the Russians – remain flash points, if not political litmus tests, to this very day. What is *not* debatable, however, is that an astonishing group of American writers emerged during these years: Norman Mailer, Saul Bellow, Truman Capote, Ralph Ellison, William Styron, Jack Kerouac, James Baldwin, Flannery O'Connor, John Cheever, J. D. Salinger, Philip Roth, and of course, John Updike.

It would, in Hemingway's famous phrase, be "pretty to think" that a single thread binds these disparate writers into a neat package. But those looking for a single theme, a dominant tradition, a defining moment – in a word, a *key* – find simplifications rather than anything approaching the truth of complicated sociocultural phenomena. One is tempted to argue that the "thread" is Hemingway himself and that the new generation wanted, as much as anything else, to sever the cord between the bloated parody of himself that Hemingway had become and the kinds of introspective writers they hoped to be. Such a view has merit if one thinks of, say, the Saul Bellow who sniped at the outmoded, overly stylized Hemingway hero in the opening pages of his 1944 novel, *Dangling Man:* "Most serious matters are closed to the hard-boiled. They are unpractised in introspection, and therefore badly equipped to deal with opponents whom they cannot shoot like big game or outdo in daring."[4]

As Bellow's quotation suggests, perhaps too much has been made of the fabled Hemingway code as it applies to characters who act, or fail to act, with a suitable "grace under pressure." For Hemingway, such defining moments usually occurred in the throes of battle, in the bullring, or on an African safari. In these extreme

– one learned to call them "existential" – situations, protagonists were tested as life and death stood in the balance. This made Hemingway enormously popular, but also made his influence problematic for writers starting out in the late 1940s. If it were true that Papa Hemingway's fabled "grace under pressure" had degenerated from an authentic portrait to a swaggering posture, it was also true that he still cast a long, intimidating shadow.

At the same time, however, there were new shadows on the horizon, and for writers starting out in the late 1950s none loomed larger or more impressively than J. D. Salinger's. *The Catcher in the Rye* not only helped to define the literary 1950s, but Holden's largely interior battle against the phonies (and perhaps himself) also ushered in an age when "innocence," rather than grace, was under pressure. Moreover, there were changes in the literary marketplace that contributed to the atmosphere surrounding Salinger's first, and only, novel. The *New Yorker* magazine (with which Salinger and later Updike are invariably linked) is probably the most important. One could argue that if Salinger had not come along when he did, bearing his tale of Holden Caulfield and later the extended saga of the Glass family, the *New Yorker* would surely have had to invent him. So right was Salinger's mixture of bright talk and brittle manners, religious quest and nervous breakdown, that it captured not only the perennial confusions of adolescence, but also the moral discomforts of an entire age. For better or worse, Holden's rebelliousness became a significant gesture in the pitched battle between conformity and opposition that would heat up considerably during the remainder of the decade.

American novels that pit Self against Society are as old as *The Scarlet Letter* or *Moby-Dick* and the list of novels that record the education of a young protagonist is both long and impressive, Goethe's *The Sorrows of Young Werther*, Joyce's *A Portrait of the Artist as a Young Man*, Lawrence's *Sons and Lovers* among them. But none of these works painted rebellion with such immediacy, or with such an infectious voice. Only *Adventures of Huckleberry Finn*, the novel to which *The Catcher in the Rye* is most often compared, seemed its equal and in the 1950s it was easier to identify with Manhattan streets and prep school mores than with small town life along the Mississippi. For younger readers, Holden was "one of them" in ways that Ishmael or Isabel Archer, Stephen Dedalus or Paul Morel – for all their literary merit – were not. When he rebelled against all that was "phony," all that made life both sad and adult, he was playing their song.

Moreover, Holden spoke to an age that not only weighed the benefits of affluence against the costs of accommodation, but that was formed by such new publishing phenomena as the mass marketing of paperback books (launched during World War II as "pocket books," in an effort to give our GIs reading material that was more flexible and that took up less space than hardcover editions) and the burgeoning book club business. *The Catcher in the Rye* began its long career as a midsummer selection of the Book-of-the-Month Club (complete with a dust jacket photo of Salinger in a tweed sports coat, holding a pipe, and looking for all the world like the sensitive young author he, in fact, was; he insisted that the photograph be deleted from subsequent editions of the novel).

The age included as well a dramatic increase in those attending our nation's colleges and universities and dramatic changes in the ways they were taught to read literature. These two factors may seem unrelated, but I would argue that burgeoning enrollments fostered by the GI Bill and the triumph of pedagogical texts such as Brooks and Warren's enormously popular *Understanding Fiction* (with its New Critical emphasis on structure, irony, and perhaps most of all, close reading of the work) created an atmosphere quite unlike any American students had experienced before. It not only made academic journals such as *College English* and *Modern Fiction Studies* possible, but more important, it made a place in the classroom for such patently "subversive" works as *The Catcher in the Rye* and *Invisible Man* (1952), for Kerouac's *On the Road* (1957) and Ginsburg's "Howl," and for *Rabbit, Run.* The age may have seemed homogeneous, but its preferred reading certainly was not.

Not all the cultural rebellions we associate with the 1950s were strictly literary. One thinks, for example, of the James Dean who taught an entire generation how to dress and mutter in films like *Rebel Without a Cause* (1955) or of the Norman O. Brown whose *Life Against Death* (1959) celebrated the therapeutic value of the polymorphous perverse. Mainstream America may have muddled through the decade wearing white bucks and watching "Leave It to Beaver," but the times were a-changin' well before Bob Dylan brought the fact to our attention a decade later. As Lowell freely, even proudly, admits in "Skunk Hour": "My mind's not right."[5] The same thing might said of the decade itself.

Hindsight has enormous advantages not given to those caught up in the whirligig of unfolding history. During the 1950s a revival of what can only be called "Victorian respectability" made domesticity seem not only attractive, but downright desirable. Thus, the decade was marked by plummeting divorce rates and a significant rise in births, by a sense that organization men were in the boardroom, women were in appliance-filled kitchens, and Eisenhower (if not God Himself) was in Washington, smiling benignly at it all.

Social historians can add a welter of detail to this general outline, but they cannot tell us what it felt like to be formed by the fifties, a decade in which young men equated marriage with the respectability, the manhood, they so desperately sought, and who imagined pregnancy was the dream only to discover that children were the nightmare. For that, I would argue, one turns to social realists like John Updike and Philip Roth.

Roth's ongoing saga of Nathan Zuckerman,[6] which evokes the ways an artist formed by literary modernism is surprised, and then bushwhacked, by life, and John Updike's decade-by-decade chronicle of Harry ("Rabbit") Angstrom, a man simultaneously formed by, and rebelling against, mass culture, are two striking examples of social realism's newer possibilities. In both cases we have come very far from the predictable aesthetics and wooden prose that characterize the social realism of, say, James T. Farrell's Studs Lonigan trilogy. We have, also, the decided advantage of seeing a single character moving against the backdrop of a larger social landscape.

No two authors, no two protagonists, could be more unlike. Roth frets about the responsibilities that force a writer to choose between one's heritage and one's art; Updike casts a theological eye on a Christianity in sharp decline. Zuckerman cannot write without looking over his shoulder and constantly assessing how his situation differs from, and often parodies, modernist giants such as Joyce, Chekhov, and James; Rabbit keeps his eyes on the television screen and his ears attuned to AM radio. Nonetheless, what strikes me as remarkable is that both authors plot their respective characters on a spread sheet beginning in the mid-1950s and continuing through the 1980s, and share a conviction about the inextricable relationship of social realism and American reality.

Roth's latest fictions – *The Counterlife* (1987), *The Facts* (1988), and *Deception* (1990) – fairly ache to be read as exercises in deconstruction, but the dazzling footwork is only partly about fictionality. Roth sees in the death of Zuckerman's parents (and his own) and in the erosion of Newark's ethnic Jewish neighborhoods the disintegration of the very material that makes for a writer's world. Roth has been playing out an elaborate end game for some time now, treading a paper-thin line separating Zuckerman from himself. One wonders how long our interest can continue.

Updike, however, makes it clear that Rabbit Angstom will not be lugging his pot belly and damaged heart into a fifth novel. What began as "Ace in the Hole," an early *New Yorker* story about a fading ex-basketball star, eventually became a lyrically textured, ersatz-sociological investigation of American reality from the mid-fifties to the present. For better or worse, Rabbit is our Everyman. He is *us*. His inclination toward irresponsibility – and his failed rebellion – are our own, writ unflinchingly large. One need not have an advanced degree in psychology to write Rabbit off as irresponsible and self-centered, immature and impossibly selfish, nor is one required to be a card-carrying feminist to realize that he will never be confused with the likes of Alan Alda or Phil Donahue. Even those uncertain about their politics would probably agree that no matter which way one turns him, he ends up looking socio-politically incorrect. Rabbit is no hero; he is not even a likable antihero. But all that said, something about Rabbit's ill-fated rebellion sticks.

Such ambivalence generates more questions than it answers. Why have we become so fascinated with the long arc of Rabbit's quest for greatness lost? Is it perhaps because no American really believes that he or she is "average" and that the mundane, quotidian life is *all?* Or does such rebellion represent the second chance, third, even fourth chance that America has offered to those who first gazed on what Fitzgerald called "a fresh green breast of the new world," a continent big enough, unspoiled enough, to be commensurate with the power of wonderment. Isn't the protagonist of *Rabbit, Run* precisely what Emerson had in mind when he talked about the transcendental Self – shining, radiant, altogether imperial – locked inside the most inconspicuous heart? Isn't it – as Ruth Leonard, the semi-professional prostitute who becomes Harry's lover in *Rabbit, Run,* puts it – because in his own stupid way, Rabbit is "still fighting"? (92)

I raise these issues not to belabor the ways in which the Rabbit tetralogy slips easily within the folds of American literature, but because Updike's detractors often count up the references to popular culture – from newspapers and magazines to radio and television – and conclude that he says far too much about far too little. One would be hard pressed to think of a subject, however inconsequential, which Updike's prose would *not* tinge with purple. As Alfred Chester, one of Updike's earliest reviewers, put it: "A God who has allowed a writer to lavish such craft upon these worthless tales is capable of anything."[7] And yet, which contemporary American writer gets us closer to the grit of surface reality, and more important, to the subtle ways that objects and emotions interact? Here, for example, is a representative sample from Rabbit Angstrom's stream of consciousness. He has left Janice and is "on the road" when he approaches a sign for ROUTE 100 WEST CHESTER WILMINGTON. He associates Wilmington with the Du Ponts, and the Du Ponts with sexual fantasy:

> A barefoot Du Pont. Brown legs probably, bitty birdy breasts. Beside a swimming pool in France. Something like money in a naked woman, deep, millions. You think of millions as being white. Sink all the way in softly still lots left. Rich girls frigid? Nymphomaniacs? Must vary. Just women after all, descended from some old Indian-cheater luckier than the rest, inherit the same stuff if they lived in a slum. Glow all the whiter there, on drab mattresses. That wonderful way they have of coming forward around you when they want it. Otherwise just fat weight. Funny how the passionate ones are often tight and dry and the slow ones wet. They want you up and hard on their little ledge. The thing is play them until just a touch. You can tell: their skin under the fur gets all loose like a puppy's neck. (26)

James Joyce once boasted that if Dublin were ever destroyed, it could be rebuilt using the pages of *Ulysses* as a blueprint. The same thing might be said of Updike's Brewer (Reading, Pennsylvania). Joycean echoes are nearly as pervasive in the Rabbit books as they are in the Zuckerman chronicles, but with some important differences: Roth measures his circumstances in terms of their distance from High Art (thus, Zuckerman may think of himself as a latter-day Stephen Dedalus, eternal son, and artistic rebel, but others keep reminding him that he is a nice Jewish boy from Newark). Updike ties his fate as a writer to the fate of the nation, and as cultural minutiae swirl through Rabbit's stream of consciousness, he becomes, in effect, Leopold Bloom's American cousin.

Updike does not call attention to the literary parallel, but if there is a touch of the artist about Rabbit's musing, much of the credit surely belongs to Bloom, simultaneously Dublin's most ordinary of ordinary citizens and modernist culture's most intriguing case study. How else can one account for such [Leopold] Bloomian passages as this one: "His thigh slides over hers, weight on warmth. Wonderful, women, from such hungry wombs to such amiable fat; he wants the heat his groin gave given back in gentle ebb. Best bedfriend, fucked woman" (87).

Or this that looks for all the world as if Ruth Leonard has lifted a leaf from Molly Bloom's famous soliloquy:

> They seemed sort of vague . . . wanting some business their wives wouldn't give, a few army words or a whimper or that business with the mouth. That. What do they see in it? It can't be as deep, she doesn't know. After all it's no worse than them at your bees and why not be generous, the first time it was Harrison and she was drunk as a monkey anyway but when she woke up the next morning wondered what the taste in her mouth *was*. . . . The thing was, they wanted to be admired there. They really did want that. They weren't that ugly but they thought they were. That was the thing that surprised her in high school how ashamed they were really, how grateful they were if you just touched them there and how quick word got around that you would. What did they think, they were monsters? If you'd just thought they might have known you were curious too, that you could like that strangeness there like they liked yours, no worse than women in their way, all red wrinkles, my God, what was it in the end? No mystery. That was

> the great thing she discovered, that it was no mystery, just a stuck-on-looking bit that made them king and if you went along with it could be good and anyway put you with them against those others, those little snips running around her at hockey in gym like a cow in that blue uniform like a baby suit she wouldn't wear it in the twelfth grade and took the demerits. (146–7)

Updike has long been regarded as a *stylist* – by those who use the word in praise, as well as by those who make it clear that the term is at best a left-handed compliment. In this regard, the Rabbit books are often seen as more evidence (as if any were needed) that a stylistic tail wags the Updike dog. What this view leaves out, however, is virtually everything that makes the Rabbit tetralogy distinctive, and I would argue, culturally important. For as we follow the arc of Rabbit's disaffection from one decade to another, style becomes as much a benchmark of "where we were" as the references to the first space walk and *2001*, the gas lines of the mid-seventies, or the air disaster over Lockerbie. Updike's selection of "facts" may serve to remind us of the TV shows we watched or the tunes that were once played on what was known as "Your Hit Parade," but what remains after the dust of cultural trivia settles is the imprint, the pattern, the *style,* if you will, that, taken together, give us a powerful sense of American "reality."

Small wonder that Rabbit finds himself spiritually restless in the 1950s, that he is perplexed by the new politics of the sixties, that visions of Krugerrands dance 'round his head in the seventies, that he winters in a Florida condominium during the 1980s. After all, Rabbit had worried early about entropy, about the "kids [who] keep coming," crowding you up, and out; in the decades that follow, Rabbit will come to feel the full force of his obsolescence and his mortality. The cumulative effect is clear. As the century winds down, so does Rabbit – and therein lies the essential difference between the literary modernists who crowed about making it NEW in a century whose birth often coincided with their own, and a writer like Updike who made his debut at the century's midpoint. Exhaustion – though hardly the sort that Barth attributes to the conventional novel[8] – may help to explain why Rabbit turns both nostalgic and politically conservative. No doubt readers of a certain age will understand and those who are not, will not.

At this point, let me narrow the focus to *Rabbit, Run,* and the formalist assumptions that went into the making of its protagonist. I have long suspected that Harry ("Rabbit") Angstrom is an extended profile of what Updike might have become had he stayed in Shillington, Pennsylvania, married a local girl, and lived out his life as dozens of his classmates actually did. Updike's mother (a tough-minded woman named Grace) apparently had other plans for her talented son, including a Harvard education and a writing career to make up for the one she had largely abandoned as a Shillington hausfrau. Moreover, Updike's classmates tell me, Grace was not above nipping potential Janice Springers in the bud to make her vicarious dream come true. In this sense, Rabbit has the character of an alternative reality, what Roth might call a "counterlife."

At the same time, however, Updike's persona suggests a complicated network of models, associations, and subtle encodings. We know, for example, that Updike's childhood nickname was "Rabbit" – for the rabbitlike way his nose twitched – but there is little doubt that the term is also meant to suggest Harry's sexual proclivities. *Angstrom* has rich possibilities as well – everything from "angstrom unit" as a measure of radiation wavelengths to *angst,* indicating the "anxiety" that sets Harry into restless motion. And finally, there is Jerry Potts, the Shillington High School basketball star, who is the most likely model for the Rabbit who set scoring records in the early 1950s. My point is that Updike's protagonist is a composite designed from a variety of pieces rather than the whole cloth of autobiography, and as such, is meant to be representative rather than "confessional." Moreover, Updike himself is the product of the New Criticism; and put enormous stock not only in irony and paradox, but also in personae and strategies of aesthetic distancing. Thus, if the cultural ambience of *Rabbit, Run* is the peculiar civilization and discontents of the 1950s, its literary structure is also pure 1950s: crafted, controlled, altogether self-conscious.

The novel opens, significantly enough, as Rabbit watches youngsters strut their stuff in a pick-up basketball game. He is in his mid-twenties, eight years (that is, two high school generations) removed from a world where first-rateness was once synonymous with purity of grace. Adulthood has turned him into an interloper; he feels himself teetering between an uncomfortable voyeurism – "His standing there makes the real boys feel strange. Eyeballs slide," (3) – and an itch to get back into the game. Not surprisingly, the old juices win out, giving rise to a lyricism that slides easily (perhaps a bit *too* easily) from its author to his protagonist:

> Boys are playing basketball around a telephone pole with a backboard bolted to it. Legs, shouts. The scrape and snap of Keds on loose alley pebbles seems to catapult their voices high into the moist March air blue above the wires. Rabbit Angstrom coming up the alley in a business suit, stops and watches, though he's twenty-six and six three. So tall, he seems an unlikely rabbit, but the breadth of white face, the pallor of his blue irises, and a nervous flutter under his brief nose as he stabs a cigarette into his mouth partially explain the nickname, which was given to him when he too was a boy. He stands there thinking, the kids keep coming, they keep crowding you up. (3)

Out of place in his double-breasted cocoa suit and other trappings of adulthood, Rabbit imagines the boys wondering if he is a pervert, poised "to offer them cigarettes or money to go out in back of the ice plant with him?" (4). But if he is older, he is not yet damaged goods: "He sinks shorts one-handed, two-handed, underhanded, flatfooted, and out of the pivot, jump, and set. Flat and soft the ball lifts. That his touch still lives in his hands elates him. He feels liberated from long gloom" (5–6).

Janice Springer Angstrom is the "long gloom" personified. Rabbit may write her off as a "dumb mutt," but the characterization (sometimes used in mock affection, sometimes in genuine disgust) doesn't square with the squalid domestic scene Updike so painstakingly details: a living room littered with toys and Old-fashioned glasses, a blaring television set, a pregnant wife. A single paragraph is enough to establish all that separates the fastidious Rabbit from his sloppy spouse:

> Carefully *he* unfolds his coat and goes to the closet with it and takes out a wire hanger. The closet is in the living-room and the door only opens half-way, since the television set is in front of it. He is careful not to kick the wire, which is plugged into a socket on the side of the door. One time Janice, who is especially clumsy when pregnant or drunk, got the wire wrapped around her foot and nearly

> pulled the set, a hundred and forty-nine dollars, down smash on the floor. Luckily he got to it while it was still rocking in the metal cradle and before Janice began kicking out in one of her panics. . . . With loving deftness, a deftness as complimentary to the articulation of his own body as to the objects he touches, he inserts the corners of the hanger into the armholes of the coat and with his long reach hangs it on the painted pipe with his other clothes. (8)

Rabbit strikes us initially as a would-be perfectionist whose life is at odds with its messy circumstances. We learn, for example, that he "never fouled" as a high school basketball player; that he regards his father's ink-stained, printer's hands as a badge of dishonor; that he takes enormous satisfaction in a fresh pair of suntans and clean shirt. He is, in short,

> the only person around here who cares about neatness. The clutter behind him in the room – the Old-fashioned glass with its corrupt dregs, the choked ashtray balanced on the easy-chair arm, the rumpled rug, the floppy stacks of slippery newspapers, the kid's toys here and there broken and stuck and jammed, a leg off a doll and a piece of bent cardboard that went with some breakfast-box cutout, the rolls of fuzz under the radiators, the continual crisscrossing mess – clings to his back like a tightening net. (14)

If the netting of a basketball hoop liberates, the domestic net tightens, and then chokes. So, when Rabbit chucks his pack of cigarettes into a garbage can (no more shortness of breath for him!) I suspect that health-conscious 1990s readers cheer their approval. After all, Updike's fading hero means to clean up his act, to make a fresh start. Others, however, may have their doubts, especially the drunken Janice when she asks him for a cigarette:

> "Huh? On the way home I threw my pack into a garbage can! I'm giving it up." He wonders how anybody could think of smoking with his stomach on edge the way it is.
>
> Janice looks at him at last. "You threw it into a garbage can! Holy Mo. You can't drink, now you don't smoke. What are you doing, becoming a saint?"(9)

Janice's question – intended as sarcasm – is at once a foreshadowing of Rabbit's bungled quest for perfection and the symptom of a larger cultural condition. During the 1950s Updike was hardly alone in exploring the connections between religion and literature.

One thinks of writers such as J. D. Salinger, Flannery O'Connor, and Bernard Malamud, and of the critics who counted up their Christ figures and mythic patterns. Given the high correlation between what critics hunt for and what they find it is hardly surprising that Rabbit Angstrom should turn out to be yet another Grail Knight/Christ figure running – ah: running – through a spiritually empty waste land. Note this selection from Joyce Markle's *Fighters and Lovers,* a book that makes no bones about seeing Rabbit as an avatar of Christ:

> For Western culture Jesus Christ is the archetypal mystic. He described himself as not of this world and sought to turn people's concerns upward, placing less importance on mundane involvements. The bible says that Peter was requested to leave his fishing (although he was married and therefore a provider) and follow Christ. Christ used the lilies of the field and the birds of the air as examples to restore people's awareness of the larger cosmos – like Mrs. Smith's garden – in which they are not their own ultimate providers.
>
> Ruth says that Rabbit thinks he is Jesus Christ, and when Rabbit goes to Eccles' house he looks at a picture of Christ and sees his own face reflected in the glass. Rabbit promises Ruth the first night, "I am a lover." Mystics are lovers, lovers of the greatest of Beloveds and ultimately lovers of humanity because they attempt to give people the greatest of gifts: a restoration of their relationship with God in which they would become special and infinitely lovable. There is a well-known book about Christ entitled *This Magnificent Lover;* the title itself describes this aspect of mystics. At the end Ruth says to Rabbit, "You love being married to everybody."[9]

Such analyses, I hasten to add, are not wildly off the mark. As discussions of Rabbit's (and Updike's) Protestantism multiply, however, one wonders if the solemn talk about Rabbit-as-saint rather misses the novel's essential point – that Rabbit's sexual urges and his religious feelings are so intertwined they are virtually identical, and that what often passes for a mystical inclination looks for all the world like selfishness. Mary Gordon puts the blame for encouraging "pseudotheological categories" squarely on Updike's shoulders. "He elevates what is essentially a physical characteristic – Rabbit's ability to enjoy life as long as no one asks anything of him, as if life were a meal, or a swim in a hospitable sea – into a spiritual virtue. Instead of settling for portraying Rabbit as a lovable forked thing, Updike insists that we see him as a kind of suburban John of the Cross."[10]

It might be well to remind ourselves that *Rabbit, Run* is about the tricky business of balancing the costs of a messy marriage against the costs of a messy flight. As the Paul Simon song "Fifty Ways to Leave Your Lover" suggests, there are at least four dozen plus variations on Rabbit's theme, but that was hardly true in the 1950s, when, Paul Anka reminds us, "Breaking Up is Hard to Do." One might argue that Rabbit chooses to "slip out the back, Jack" at the point when he can no longer bear the pregnant, sloppy Janice: "Janice is a frightening person. Her eyes dwindle in their frowning sockets and her little mouth hands over in a dumb slot. Since her hair has begun to thin back from her shiny forehead, he keeps getting the feeling of her being brittle, and immovable, of her only going one way, toward deeper wrinkles and skimpier hair" (10–11). One need not be a pinchfaced feminist to feel that this is scarcely the stuff that love – be it Christian, mystical, or just plain human – is made of.

Not surprisingly, Rabbit insists that he abandoned Janice for other, nobler reasons: "I once did something right. I played first–rate basketball. I really did. And after you're first-rate at something, no matter what, it kind of takes the kick out of being second-rate. And that little thing Janice and I had going was really second-rate" (106–7). In Paul Simon's words, he got "a new plan, Stan" – and one, moreover, that takes the full measure of his individualism into account: "When I ran from Janice I made an interesting discovery. . . . If you have the guts to be yourself . . . other people'll pay your price" (149).

Rabbit, Run tests the strength of Rabbit's radical Emersonianism against the power of cultural nets. No doubt some would argue that the novel ends by affirming the power of the Self, with Rabbit still on his feet and still running; others, however, will be quick to point out that he not only "returns," but also hangs around for three decades and three more novels. I suspect there are those who would argue that the contest between Self and Society ends in a draw. My hunch is that Rabbit has as little luck figuring out where he wants to go as he does in articulating the "it" he is searching for, and that this is as true for *Rabbit, Run* as for the tetralogy bearing his name. Still, in the 1950s, one could get into one's car and go – that is, if the "one" in question were a male. Presumably, most female counterparts (such as Thelma and Louise) would have to wait until the 1990s.

About some matters, however, we can be certain. Rabbit leaves Janice on a date readers can fix with precision: Friday, March 20, 1959.[11] Moreover, his circular route, from Brewer to Lancaster to Frederick, Maryland, and return, is rendered with the exactness to quotidian detail that has become Updike's trademark. But that said, what one reads even more clearly is the futility of Rabbit's flight. He is no Kerouac "on the road"; he is not even a Huck imagining (wrongly) an unfettered, pastoral life in the Indian Territories. Rather, Rabbit drifts, unsure of his purpose, much less its direction. He may be what Brewer, Pennsylvania, regards as a rebel (in their Pennsylvania Dutch, *schussel*), but he is small potatoes compared to those American protagonists who followed Natty Bumppo over the next hill.

Updike drives home the point by having a gnarled gas station attendant (read wise old man) put it to him this way: "Son, where do you want to go?" (27). Rabbit cannot answer his question; neither the man's directions nor the AAA's best road map will suffice. Moreover, Rabbit's overly active, guilt-ridden imagination concocts a scenario in which the police are about to be called and Rabbit exposed as a "criminal": "he [the gas station attendant] disappears into the hardware store; maybe he's phoning the state cops. He acts like he knows something" (28). It turns out that he has managed to scare up a New York State road map, but also figures that is not where Rabbit is headed.

> "No," Rabbit answers, and walks back to his car door. He feels through the hairs on the back of his neck the man following him. He gets into the car and slams the door and the farmer is right there, the meat of his face hung in the open door window. He bends down and nearly sticks his face in. His cracked thin lips with a scar tilting toward his nose move thoughtfully. He is wearing glasses, a scholar. "The only way to get somewhere, you know, is to figure out where you're going before you go there." (28)

Mary Gordon argues otherwise, insisting that, for the bulk of American literature's male protagonists, motion is what matters: "The image of the moving boy has been central in American writing. Motion is the boy's genius. He *must* be able to move.... And fate's agent, the embodiment of unmoving weight, is female. She who does not move, who will not move, who cannot move. Who won't allow the boy to move."[12] Given the sheer importance of running in a novel entitled *Rabbit, Run,* the case for motion seems self-evident, but something in Gordon's formulation doesn't ring quite true – or perhaps true enough – for Updike's work. If motion defines Rabbit, the reasons include more, much more, than the simple (reductive?) fact that he is a white American male.

Gordon is a *rara avis,* an articulate (read: readable) intellectual whose feminist agenda is rooted in genuine moral passion. She is a wordsmith to reckon with. By contrast, language is not the best medium for Rabbit's message. He prefers the remembrance of basketball games past (the county scoring record he set in 1950 and then broke in 1951; the cider jug passed around after the Oriole High game) and the way the sheer exhilaration of knowing he was "on" squares with what Marty Tothero, his high school coach, now calls "the *sacredness* of accomplishment" (62). Both coach and player have declined since the halcyon days when "grace" was defined as effortless running and pure shooting, but Rabbit, unlike Tothero, has not given up on the possibilities of purity.

Enter Jack Eccles, an early instance in the long line of church failures who populate Updike's fiction. That his name suggests affinities to the Koheleth of the Book of Ecclesiastes is true enough, although we are also reminded that Leopold and Molly Bloom share an ironic "abode of bliss" at 7 Eccles Street, Dublin. No doubt Updike wants the name game to cut both ways, but if *vanity* is the charged word of the former and an *ennobled ordinariness* the earmark of the latter, what can we say of their contemporary counterpart? Eccles is clearly more comfortable in his role as social worker than as minister, less threatened by those in his youth group who worry about the religious implications of mid-level petting than he is by a wife who spouts Freudian psychology and wields a symbolically castrating knife. Most of all, however, Eccles worries about the God that, for him, remains more idea than immanent, mystical presence.

The result is a curious reversal of roles, with Rabbit "ministering" to Eccles quite as much as Eccles ministers to Rabbit. Not surprisingly, Eccles prefers to do his pastoring on the golf course. And in a scene that reverberates throughout the tetralogy, Eccles and Rabbit take turns swatting at the ball as they debate theology:

> "Harry," he asks, sweetly yet boldly, "why have you left her? You're obviously deeply involved with her."
>
> "I *told* ya. There was this thing that wasn't there."
>
> "What thing? Have you ever seen it? Are you sure it exists?"
>
> Harry's two-foot putt dribbles short and he picks up the ball with trembling fingers. "Well, if you're not sure it exists don't ask me. It's up your alley. If you don't know nobody does."
>
> "No," Eccles cries in the same strained voice in which he told his wife to keep her heart open for Grace. "Christianity isn't looking for a rainbow. If it were what you think it is we'd pass out opium at services. We're trying to *serve* God, not *be* God. . . ."
>
> "I tell you, I know what it is." (133)

What follows can only be called an epiphanic moment, one not unlike the "purity of line" that Hemingway uses to describe Romero, the young bullfighter in *The Sun Also Rises,* or the magical moment Updike captures in "Kid Bids Hub Fans Adieu," an account of Ted Williams swatting a home run at his last trip to the plate:

> In avoiding looking at Eccles he looks at the ball, which sits high on the tee and already seems free of the ground. Very simply he brings the clubhead around his shoulder into it. The sound has a hollowness, a singleness he hasn't heard before. His arms force his head up and his ball is hung way out, lunarly pale against the beautiful black blue of storm clouds, his grandfather's color stretched dense across the east. It recedes, star, speck. It hesitates, and Rabbit thinks it will die, but he's fooled, for the ball makes this hesitation the ground of a final leap: with a kind of visible solo take a last bit of space before vanishing in falling. "That's *it!*" he cries and, turning to Eccles with a smile of aggrandizement, repeats, "That's it." (134)

Mysticism begins in a stubborn refusal to recognize quotidian reality as *all,* and generally goes on to insist that heightened experiences – long, solitary sojourns in the desert, for example – can make the metaphysical palpable, if not bring it into reach. For Rabbit, the perfect golf shot, like the well-arched basketball, is an intimation of the transcendental, a moment of such aching grace that it exists wholly, purely, unto itself – outside the realm of the conventional, the mundane, the capacity of an Eccles to understand.

Thus, Rabbit's ecstatic "That's *it!*" is simultaneously discovery and confirmation, a moment when confusion gives way to wordless certainty. Morever, this all-important *It* conflates God, the motions of grace, the pure camaraderie of sport, and perhaps most important of all, the bracing possibility of a new, pristine chance at the next tee into a single image. Rabbit's epiphany on the links ends the chapter, but some thirty years – and three Rabbit books later – Updike provides a lyrical gloss on what golf has come to mean to the Rabbit who once defined his spiritual being on the basketball court:

> [I]n golf, the distances, the hundreds of yards, dissolve to a few effortless swings if you find the inner magic, the key. Always, weightlessness and consummate ease, for now and again it does happen, happens in three dimensions, shot after shot. But then he gets human and tries to force it, to make it happen, to get ten extra yards, to steer it, and it goes away, grace you could call it, the feeling of collaboration, of being bigger than he really is. When you stand up on the first tee it is there, it comes back from wherever it lives during the rest of your life, endless possibility, the possibility of a flawless round, a round without a speck of dirt on it, without a missed two-footer or a flying right elbow, without a pushed wood or pulled iron; the first fairway is in front of you, palm trees on the left and water on the right, flat as a picture. All you have to do is take a simple pure swing and puncture the picture in the middle with a ball that shrinks in a second to the size of a needle-prick, a tiny tunnel into the absolute. That would be it.[13]

Indeed, one could argue that the Rabbit tetralogy is a story of how Harry Angstrom keeps faith with this dream of an unsullied "it" even as the social landscape around him darkens and the costs of his selfishness continue to mount. *Rabbit, Run* has the advantage of laying out the pieces of Rabbit's psychological profile in bold relief. For however much he is attracted to versions of "flight" (he muses on at least fifty ways to burst out of the domestic net, and acts on several of them), he seems equally drawn to modes of return.

Notice, for example, how Rabbit's smug victory over the exasperated Eccles at the golf course is followed by a paean to Rabbit as grail knight in the waste land of Mrs. Smith's ailing rhododendrons: "Sun and moon, sun and moon, time goes. In Mrs. Smith's acres, crocuses break the crust. Daffodils and narcissi unpack their trumpets" (135). In this world where the echoes to Eliot's *The Waste Land* are as obvious as they are sometimes deafening, where April is compassionate and cruel, Updike's protagonist/antihero is simultaneously Mr. Life and Mr. Death. As Mrs. Smith would have it, Rabbit is a force without history, without cultural baggage; he arrives, as mythic heroes always do, from an offstage "nowhere," bearing redemption:

> "It's been a religious duty to me, to keep Horace's garden up. . . . I won't be here next year to see Harry's rhodies come in again. You kept me alive, Harry; it's the truth; you did. All winter I was fighting the grave and then in April I looked out the window and here was this tall young man burning my old stalks and I knew life hadn't left me. That's what you have, Harry: life. It's a strange gift and I don't know how we're supposed to use it but I know it's the only gift we get and it's a good one." (224)

The no-nonsense, hard-boiled Ruth Leonard argues otherwise: Rabbit is "Mr. Death himself" – not just nothing, but "worse than nothing" (304). Both employer and paramour, I would argue, have touched a side of Rabbit's complicated truth. Moreover, these competing assessments not only have crossed Rabbit's consciousness, but they also account for the cultural configuration of his erratic motion. For a part of Rabbit takes heart from the "specialness" of his destiny (he is, after all, a first-rater unwilling to accept gradations downward); that others must pay the price is, ironically enough, *his* price as well. If teammates such as Ronnie Harrison had to learn to accept Rabbit's ball-hogging on the basketball court, *he* had to make the shots that won them championships; if Janice and Ruth find themselves on the receiving end of Rabbit's sexual urges, he also pays a heavy toll in the coin of guilt. What the others fail to see is how spiritual all this is, how everything from washing Ruth's overly made-up face to racing back to Janice's hospital bedside is tangled around God's fearful omnipresence and the dark certainties of death. Rabbit is simultaneously attracted and repulsed by the theological images he cannot *not* collect:

> Harry has no taste for the dark, tangled, visceral aspect of Christianity, the going *through* quality of it, the passage *into* death and suffering that redeems and inverts these things, like an umbrella blowing inside out. He lacks the mindful will to walk the straight line of a paradox. His eyes turn toward the light however it glances into his retina. (237)

What Rabbit desperately seeks is nothing more or less than the "good home," the secure place, that has thus far eluded him – and this (ironically, paradoxically) never more so than when he seems most bent on slipping through domestic nets with the effortless swish of a basketball. What he discovers, of course, is that adult life lacks the certainty, the purity, of childhood games. Rather, it is often a messy, tangled affair. For example, in the hospital waiting room, Rabbit adds a heavy dose of "consequence" to the older arithmetic of rationalization:

> He is certain that as a consequence of his sin Janice or the baby will die. His sin is a conglomerate of flight, cruelty, obscenity, and conceit; a black clot embodied in the entrails of the birth. . . . His idea grows, that it will be a monster, a monster of his making. The thrust whereby it was conceived becomes confused in his mind with the perverted entry a few hours ago he made into Ruth. Momentarily drained of lust, he stares at the remembered contortions to which it had driven him. His life seems a sequence of grotesque poses assumed to no purpose, a magic dance empty of belief. *There is no God; Janice can die;* the two thoughts come at once, in one slow wave. He feels underwater, caught in chains of transparent slime, ghosts of the urgent ejaculations he has spat into the mild bodies of women. (196–8)

For better or worse, Rabbit is every bit as much a victim of the "biological trap" as Freud insisted women were; and when the siren calls of lust fill his ears, he responds on a purely animal level. The limp rationalizations that follow – whether vested in aspects of "specialness" and/or domestic squalor – are predictable and, given Rabbit, perhaps understandable, but they do not convince. For all its social realism *Rabbit, Run* is finally less about what Pascal's epigraph calls "external circumstances" than about Rabbit's self-stylized runner's high: an ecstasy so intensely narcissistic that only the "motions of Grace" can release its full power:

> Goodness lies inside, there is nothing outside, those things he was trying to balance have no weight. He feels his inside as very real suddenly, a pure blank space in the middle of a dense net. . . . His hands lift of their own and he feels the wind on his ears even before, his heels hitting heavily on the pavement at first but with an effortless gathering out of a kind of sweet panic growing lighter and quicker and quieter, he runs. Ah: runs. Runs. (308–9)

Rabbit's "sweet panic" – like Lowell's "tranquilized fifties" – is a lively emblem of the decade, for it manages to yoke conformity with rebellion, the thick textures of social realism with splashes of the transcendental. The culture of the 1950s embraced both possibilities, sometimes emphasizing one, sometimes the other. Not surprisingly, its best, most representative literary works – and I would count *Rabbit, Run* among them – were the products of a bifurcated, often deeply ambivalent vision. Thus, Rabbit seeks security at one point, radical independence at another. Such were the symptomatic behaviors of the 1950s, an instance, if you will, of what W. H. Auden meant when he declared that love and freedom were (alas) incompatible.

Those of us who first encountered *Rabbit, Run* in 1960 were not wrong in imagining that Rabbit would be lugging his problems and his muttlike spouse through at least one more novel. As a fellow Pennsylvanian, one who had read Updike's Olinger stories as they came out, story after story, in the pages of the *New Yorker,* I felt a particular kinship to the world of farms and small towners he described – despite the fact that I grew up in a nondescript Western Pennsylvania town that had more slag heaps, coal mines, and glass factories than versions of the pastoral. I "identified" (for want of a better word) with the world that produced a Rabbit Angstrom because, for better or worse, I could see his fading glory reflected in the faces of my former classmates.

Rabbit turned out to be one of contemporary American literature's more durable protagonists; the problems he faced during the next decades tell us much about how and why the culture changed. But the Rabbit of *Rabbit, Run* retains a fascination that even the richest of the subsequent novels never quite matched; he was, as William Faulkner once said of Caddy Compson, our "heart's darling," the source of our deepest dreams of radical independence and our darkest nightmare lest our prayers be answered.

NOTES

1 John Updike, *Rabbit, Run* (New York: Alfred A. Knopf, 1960; rev. and rpt. 1970). Page references in the text are to the 1970 reprint.

2 In "The Rabbit Tetralogy: From Solitude to Society to Solitude Again" (*Modern Fiction Studies* [Spring 1991]), Matthew Wilson sees *Rabbit, Run* as "typical of what Robert Lowell called the 'tranquilized *Fifties,*' a time of conformity and of national somnolence," and Rabbit as a character "so self-involved that he is not aware (as he is in later novels) of participating in or reflecting any national trends." I would argue that Lowell's phrase is both darker and more problematic than Wilson suggests. Although Rabbit is certainly "self-involved," I see him as an accurate, albeit exaggerated, barometer of the decade's deeply ambivalent attitudes about responsibility, respectability, and most of all, marriage.

3 Irving Howe, *Selected Writings, 1950–1990* (New York: Harcourt Brace Jovanovich, 1990), p. 35.

4 Saul Bellow, *Dangling Man* (New York: Vanguard, 1944), p. 3.

5 Robert Lowell, *Life Studies* (New York: Farrar Straus & Giroux, 1959), p. 90.

6 Philip Roth, *My Life as a Man* (New York: Holt, Rinehart and Winston, 1974).

7 Alfred Chester, Review of *Pigeon Feathers* (*Commonweal,* July 1962): 77–90.

8 In "The Literature of Exhaustion" (*Atlantic,* 1967), Barth defined *exhaustion* as "the used-upness of certain forms or . . . certain possibilities" and went on to suggest that "a good many current novelists write turn-of-the-century-type novels, only in more or less mid-twentieth-century language and about contemporary people and topics." To these charges an old-fashioned social realist like Updike could only plead guilty. On the other hand, the exhaustion that interests Updike has to do with matter rather than method, with the larger convulsions of a culture as opposed to the niceties of technique.

9 Joyce Markle, *Fighters and Lovers* (New York: New York University Press, 1973), p. 52.

10 Mary Gordon, *Good Boys and Dead Girls* (New York: Viking, 1991), p. 21.

11 That Rabbit listens to news bulletins about the Dalai Lama (still missing after the downfall of Tibet to the Chinese Communists) identifies the month as March, the year as 1959; a few pages later we learn that Rabbit returns from his abortive flight on a Saturday and that he and Ruth Leonard "celebrate" Palm Sunday in her apartment (positioned significantly enough directly across the street from a church). In 1959, Palm Sunday fell on March 22nd.

12 Gordon, pp. 3–4.

13 John Updike, *Rabbit at Rest* (New York: Alfred A. Knopf, 1990), p. 56.

4

The Americanness of *Rabbit, Run:* A Transatlantic View

ERIK KIELLAND-LUND

THE European fascination with America is as old as America itself. Ever since the early explorers sent their tantalizing reports back to the Old World, America has been both a physical place and a mythological region of the mind. In the words of a pioneer of American studies in Europe, Sigmund Skard, "the image of the United States carried a vicarious value, positive and negative; while depicting America it came at the same time to serve and to reflect, in a curious and revealing way, the needs of the Europeans themselves."[1] From the very beginning, the dream of America was also a European dream of what life and society might become if the constraints of a stratified and largely static civilization could be left behind. Thus, from de Tocqueville to Dickens to Alistair Cooke, reflections on the American journey are not just an attempt to paint a realistic picture of the new nation, they are also an exploration of self and a testing of stereotypes and preconceptions, both general and individual.

This process has been further complicated in the postwar period by the ubiquitous presence in Europe of a wide range of products of American popular culture. The European consciousness is constantly exposed to images of American life, not just in the familiar creations of Hollywood and the omnipresent rhythms of popular music, but increasingly in soap operas and other television series, in continuous news coverage courtesy of CNN, and in the inanities of TV commercials. In the absence of a common European identity, it seems that American popular culture has to a large extent provided a frame of reference and a means of communication, especially among young people, for the contemporary European mind.[2] European readers will thus bring to the study of American literature a large number of secondhand ideas and impressions that will color their perceptions of the works in question. These perceptions will usually be far more accurate and sophisticated than the proverbial observation of the bright Third World scholar who had expected the United States to have "more of a cowboy problem."[3] Yet the gap between the mythical America in every European's mind and the real United States may still be large and will necessarily put a personal stamp on the particular "Americanness" ascertainable in any given work. The transatlantic reader will identify in fiction the particular features and patterns that seem to him or her "typically American."

In light of the perennial European fascination with America, it is not surprising that the popularity of certain American authors will often depend on their ability to create a world that seems palpably real in its American particulars. In the case of John Updike, his stature in Europe as one of the most accomplished and interesting of modern authors has much to do with his impressive ability to describe such American realities. When *Rabbit, Run* was first published in the United States in 1960, its author was unknown to Europeans, except for the small band of America watchers who subscribed to the *New Yorker*. The novel was soon recognized as a work of major significance and was translated into eleven European languages between 1961 and 1971.[4] Widely reviewed, it was commonly seen as a fascinating if depressing exposé of many typical features of postwar America. In a Europe still emerging from the shadows of World War II and only on the brink of a new age of affluence and mass media culture, *Rabbit, Run* was recognized as being deeply rooted in such typical American characteristics as individualism, immaturity, religiosity, and love of sports, while at the same time making an important statement about the modern world in general. Many reviewers praised Updike's ability to convey not just the surface textures of the nation's experience, but also the deeper thematic and mythical substructures that define his characters and their struggles in universal terms. Thus, reading Updike from a transatlantic point of view has been, from the very beginning, a question of interpreting the events of Brewer, Pennsylvania, or Tarbox, Massachusetts, in a much larger framework of meaning. Whether it is a question of the protean permutations of the American Dream (which often come across as human dreams writ large), the confusions of sex and love, the restless search for an identity that can affirm a spiritual meaning beyond the decay of physical life, or the longing for the absolute control of the perfect jump shot, Updike's world is always made to seem both local and universal.

Rabbit, Run may have weathered the passage of time better than most novels because Updike's America of the fifties reflects enduring characteristics of American psychology and society.[5] Maybe because, as Updike himself has observed, *Rabbit, Run* was a product *of* the fifties and not really in a conscious way *about* the fifties,[6] the author has tapped into the archetypal sources of the American mind. Certainly the world of the novel is eminently recognizable from the perspective of the nineties, and what seems most striking from a transatlantic point of view, is not how much America and Americans have changed, but how much Europe has become "Americanized."[7]

The special Americanness of *Rabbit, Run* is felt from the very beginning of the novel, as Updike introduces one of its major themes. When Harry Angstrom[8] comes home from work in his business suit and involves himself in the kids' basketball game, reliving the glory days of his record-setting high school performances, we are in the presence of a special form of athletic nostalgia characteristic of a culture "hooked" on sports and its youthful heroes. Harry loses himself and his present frustration in the kids' game: "That old stretched-leather feeling makes his whole body go taut, gives his arms wings. It feels like he's reaching down through years to touch this tautness."[9]

As readers familiar with Updike's work would expect, Rabbit's sexual scoring also reflects his athletic specialness. His earliest sexual experiences with Mary Ann remain in his memory inextricably mixed with his success on the court: "He came to her as a winner and that's the feeling he's missed since. In the same way she was the best of them all because she was the one he brought most to, so tired" (198). To underline the centrality of sports in Harry's American experience even further, sports metaphors permeate his speech and thought; his religious quest is presented as a game of golf and his memories of boyhood Saturday mornings are of "the blank scoreboard of a long game about to begin" (40).

The "external circumstances" referred to in the epigraph from Pascal have a great deal to do with the presence and absence of athletic achievement in Rabbit's life. The theme of the lapsed athlete can be traced throughout *Rabbit, Run.* Harry's attempt to recapture the sensation of poise and control on the golf course may give him a few moments of "That's *it!*", but they are obviously a very poor substitute for the real thing. His tendency to talk of "the good old days" when he is out on the town is also an illustration of how much of his life is anchored in a much more desirable past. This nostalgia is part of a larger pattern, where the mediocrity of his present life with Janice is juxtaposed to his happy memories of childhood with Mim and his athletic achievements in high school. This mood of wistful nostalgia is typical of many of Updike's works, and to a European the sense of the urgency of youth and the long fall toward a pathetic middle and old age seem a particularly American attitude, which Rabbit even turns into a kind of Law of Life by observing that "the fullness ends when we give Nature her ransom, when we make children for her. Then she is through with us, and we become, first inside, and then outside, junk. Flower stalks" (226). And the speaker has reached the ripe old age of twenty-six!

Although Harry may make what is statistically a correct observation when he reflects that he married "relatively late" at twenty-four, for all practical purposes his life is in one sense closing before it has really begun.[10] Unlike Janice, Rabbit has an instinctive sense of being cut out for something very different from his current life that makes it impossible for him not to run when the walls of respectable ordinariness start to close in on him.[11] It is not just the memory of his high-flying days on the basketball court that makes him react claustrophobically during the burial scene at the end of the novel, it is also the feeling of a whole different world waiting for him on the other side of the mountain.

In these inchoate longings for a more satisfactory life beyond the norms of ordinary society, Harry Angstrom is repeating one of the most pervasive themes in American literary history, as well as acting out many of the ideals of Emersonian transcendentalism. The conflict between nature and nurture, the need to affirm desires and aspirations that society has no room for, these provide the impetus behind Huck Finn's "lighting out for the territory," Holden Caulfield's quixotic battle against "phoniness," and a host of other such impulses in major works of American fiction. Rabbit, like the Emersonian hero, chooses to listen to his own instinctive sense of what is right and wrong. He refuses to act in a "mature" way, since he believes that acceptance of his role in society is the ultimate imprisonment. As he says to Reverend Eccles: "If you're telling me I'm not mature, that's one thing I don't cry over since as far as I can make out it's the same thing as being dead" (107).

This statement goes a long way toward explaining the very common European perception that Americans retain adolescent qualities far into adulthood, whether diagnosed as the "Peter Pan syndrome" or as a part of what Europeans tend to describe as American shallowness and superficiality. This refusal of a grown-up commitment to one person, one place, or one way of life is in Rabbit's mind a necessary refusal to give up his options. This might be seen in a positive light, even by Ruth, who is so often Harry's most severe critic, when she reflects that Rabbit is about the only person she knows who still has not given up, who is still fighting (92). No doubt this is part of Rabbit's ability to make her feel special too. The trouble with such a philosophy, however, is that it presupposes an ability to go ahead in a reasonably straight line from one point to another. For Rabbit, the Sartrean "margin of freedom" where the fight for existential authenticity must be won or lost, all too often becomes "the vast blank of his freedom" (51), where he is simply lost in the fog of his own insecurity and indecisiveness.

Because Harry is incapable of philosophical analysis and understanding, he cannot, like Whitman, make joyful sense of his own predicament.[12] Nor can he, like Emerson, trust his own instincts home because they are seen as basically divinely inspired. Rabbit's intermittent intuition "that somewhere behind all this . . . there's something that wants me to find it" (120), is a very feeble descendant of Emerson's enthusiastic conviction that individual nonconformity can be given direction and purpose because self-reliance is God-reliance:

> Great men have always done so and confided themselves childlike to the genius of their age, betraying their perception that the Eternal was stirring at their heart, working through their hands, predominating in all their being.[13]

It is also in the Emersonian tradition to exalt feeling over thought, intuition over logic, and to emphasize the virtue of the expression of the spontaneous self over the norms and directives of society. But such a Romantic invitation to rebellion and self-affirmation is made much more ambiguous when society itself enlists the heart to uphold its patterns. When Eccles asks Mrs. Angstrom what her husband thinks Harry ought to do, she answers:

> Crawl back. What else? He will, too, poor boy. He's just like his father underneath. All soft heart. I suppose that's why men rule the world. They're all heart. . . . Men are all heart and women are all body. I don't know who's supposed to have the brains. God, I suppose. (161)

Because of Harry's debilitating ambivalence, he is ultimately an easy prey for those who want to enlist his guilty conscience in the service of "doing the right thing." His will to break out is never backed up by a firm and rational game plan for the achievement of freedom.

The lack of a firmly established intellectual center in Harry's life can also be seen as an aspect of the American tendency to emphasize feeling over thought, reflected in the Americans' preference for the expression "I feel" when stating a considered opinion.[14] On numerous occasions in the novel, Harry defines himself as solely a creature of instinct and feeling. After his final inexcusable treatment of Ruth, he observes that "he doesn't know why he did except it felt right at the time" (191), and when Ruth later asks him why he is so insistent that she give birth to their baby, all he can answer is: "I don't know. I don't know any of these answers. All I know is what feels right" (306). Harry Angstrom has completed a high school education, but the closest he gets to a book in the course of the novel is to look at Ruth's mysteries. His gifts of calculation go as far as counting the dwindling number of dollar bills in his wallet and his oratorical skills are enlisted in the service of the MagiPeel Peeler. No one has taught Harry how to develop a taste for intellectual achievement, and to a European reader the total lack of stimulus in this direction is one more indication of the anti-intellectualism of American middle-class culture. For whatever reason, Americans like Harry Angstrom seem deplorably incapable of sustaining habits of intellectual curiosity beyond the entertainment level of popular culture.

The ubiquity of many products of that popular culture is another important aspect of the Americanness of *Rabbit, Run*. Updike almost always anchors his novels firmly in time and place and makes clear in what season, month, and sometimes even day and minute the events of the novel take place.[15] Not just the newscast but also the popular songs Harry listens to on his car radio going south, indicate that this is the early spring of 1959. And not just to Americans, since the rock revolution of the mid-fifties meant an unprecedented exposure to American popular music in Europe. Some of the most vivid memories of the present writer go back to the late fifties, when Radio Luxembourg, "the Station of the Stars," started its transmission of the strange new sounds of American music all over Europe. "Stagger Lee" and "Venus," Lloyd Price and Frankie Avalon, these were passports to another world for a generation of young people far beyond America's shores. Even if Updike overdoes it with his long list of titles, reminiscent of a Whitmanian catalogue, perhaps this is the perfect symbolic reflection of the absent-minded tedium of driving off into nowhere, and it does provide the reader with useful cultural bearings.

Harry's spontaneous flight from his world of frustration and boredom represents one of the most typically American sequences of the novel. The flight itself, down the highways of America, is not just thematically central, reenacting the "On the Road" experience from Whitman to Kerouac. It also provides the reader, in graphic and sensuous detail, with a sense of the realities of another sphere than the one circumscribed by Brewer and Mt. Judge. The names of cities and towns, the highway numbers, the simple everyday actions of filling up with gas and eating a hamburger at the roadside diner, the new sounds and smells of another region, all add up to a satisfying density of texture that makes this sequence unmistakably American. For Europeans chiefly familiar with the United States through the images of Hollywood, there are several moments of recognition here.[16] One particularly poignant one comes when Rabbit stops at a cafe in West Virginia, right before going back to Brewer. In a cameo version of *Easy Rider*, Updike conveys to the reader the feeling of being a stranger in your own land.

> Somehow, though he can't put his finger on the difference, he is unlike the other customers. They sense it too, and look at him with hard eyes. . . . In the hush his entrance creates, the excessive courtesy the weary woman behind the counter shows him amplifies his strangeness. . . . He had thought, he had read, that from shore to shore all America was the same. He wonders, Is it just these people I'm outside, or is it all America? (33)

Here is a sense of the enduring provincialism of the great continent Rabbit inhabits, and of an alienation that seems to reflect the complexity and vastness of the nation.

In many other descriptive passages in the novel, Updike's visceral feel for the details of the American urban scene combines with his poet's vision to create passages that stay in the mind long after the reading is over. Very often they also echo the important tension in the novel, again typical of the American tradition, between nostalgic longing for a vanishing pastoral ideal and grudging acceptance of the potential beauty of the cold and metallic urban landscape:

> At the corner, where Wilbur Street meets Potter Avenue, a mailbox stands leaning in twilight on its concrete post. Tall two-petalled street-sign, the cleat-gouged trunk of the telephone pole holding its insulators against the sky, fire hydrants like a golden bush: a grove. (15)

In another memorable vignette Rabbit returns to Brewer from his abortive escape:

> He comes into Brewer from the south, seeing it in the smoky shadow before dawn as a gradual multiplication of houses among the trees beside the road and then as a treeless waste of industry, shoe fac-

> tories and bottling plants and company parking lots and knitting mills converted to electronics parts and elephantine gas tanks lifting above trash-filled swamp-land yet lower than the blue edge of the mountain from whose crest Brewer was a warm carpet woven around a single shade of brick. Above the mountain, stars fade. (39)

In such haunting scenes, depicting the landscapes of contemporary America, Updike ensures that the reader will not forget that the drama of Rabbit's life is inextricable from its setting.

Among European readers, John Updike is recognized as the great contemporary chronicler of the suburban middle classes in America, and there is a strong impression that many of his books, especially the Rabbit tetralogy, amount to a picture of "the way we live now." In this anatomy of middle-class life, the relationship between the sexes is obviously of paramount importance and informs much of *Rabbit, Run.* A full treatment of this theme clearly lies outside the scope of this essay, but certain aspects of it seem particularly American to European eyes. Most striking is the total lack of respect and solidarity in the Angstrom household. Even granted that Rabbit needs to vent his frustration with his life, and that Janice is closest at hand for this purpose, the vitriolic nature of many of his comments, some in mixed company, seems uncomfortably excessive.[17] That Janice is a "dumb mutt" appears to be one of his most cherished convictions and her pregnancy "infuriates him with its look of stubborn lumpiness" (10). Their dialogue in the beginning of the novel represents the grotesque mixture of terms of endearment and swear words all too typical of male-female relations in America. It is a striking feature of Harry's linguistic behavior that he uses profanities much less frequently than Europeans have come to expect from young American males, except when he is talking to his wife. Then the swear words strike like a barrage, creating a distance that the mechanical "I love you" cannot shrink. After Janice has said " 'You bastard' very thoughtfully," Harry counters with "Screw you," before adopting his repentance pose. Then Janice calls from the kitchen, " 'And honey pick up a pack of cigarettes, could you?' in a normal voice that says everything is forgiven, everything is the same" (11–15).

In Updike's fiction, one is always reminded how much language counts for in human life. In his fastidious respect for the nuances of meaning of each appropriately chosen word, he reminds the reader how easy it is to lose that respect when words are no longer chosen to convey the deeper truths of human perception and emotion. Ironically contrasted to the narrative precision, all the embarrassing (to a European sensibility) "darlings" and "honeys" of the dialogue and the way "I love you" comes trippingly off the tongue as a kind of linguistic reflex, exemplify the kind of language inflation that has come to seem typical of American speech habits.[18] This supports the European perception of American superficiality and the lack of a truly private sphere, an inner sanctum, where such words and the depth of feeling they are meant to convey really belong.

The American language also seems to reveal, in many of its colloquial words and expressions, a lack of respect for women. *Rabbit, Run* is not a misogynist novel, Harry is far too attracted to the female sex for that, but his respect for women as separate individuals, that do not exist solely to be lusted after and "screwed" and "nailed" by him, seems nonexistent. It is thus entirely in character when he asks Ruth to "be a pleasant piece" (74) on the way to her apartment after their first date. Clearly, the feminist revolution seems to have been more urgently needed in the United States than in many other countries! The kind of locker-room mentality displayed not just by Harry but even more offensively by Ronnie Harrison, seems embarrassingly adolescent among men who are twenty-six years old. Harry appears to be utterly incapable of relating to women without engaging in sexual fantasies. He imagines that all the women he lusts after have a corresponding desire to jump into bed with him, no matter what their marital status or how long he has known them. For Europeans used to watching American soap operas and following up on the serial relationships of film and rock stars, promiscuity appears to be as American as apple pie. In many of his other novels, Updike does even more to reinforce this impression than in *Rabbit, Run*.

This near obsession with sexuality is not just a striking feature of Harry's personality and of Updike's fiction in general, but also seems to foreign eyes the obverse side of the sway of "puritanism" in American life. Not just Lucy Eccles, but the American middle class at large have taken Freud to heart as a defense against traditional feelings of guilt and prudishness. Harry, fornicating happily with Ruth across the street from the church on Summer Street, may know that he is committing a sin according to the religion he professes to believe in, but there is no sense here of marriage being the kind of sacrament Eccles is trying to remind him of. Harry's morality seems to be utterly of this world, based on the expression of natural instincts, regardless of the consequences for other people. Nothing is more revealing than his conviction that "if you have the guts to be yourself, other people'll pay your price" (149). A further illustration of this heartless egotism can be seen in the way he keeps Ruth from using contraception because the thought of it turns him off, and in his insistence that she not have an abortion, although he has no intention of taking his fatherhood responsibilities seriously. Concern for the consequences of his actions and the people he hurts is not Rabbit's game.

As in most of Updike's other novels, religion is an important theme in *Rabbit, Run.* Unusual among modern novelists, Updike is a committed Christian, and many of his characters wrestle with the implications of their beliefs. Europeans know that Americans score much higher on "belief in God and an afterlife" and that many more go to church regularly than in most European nations. There is also, however, the impression that for Americans religion is a social rather than a doctrinal phenomenon, and that the connection between a professed belief and one's actual behavior may be problematic at best. From Elmer Gantry to Jimmy Swaggart and Jim Bakker, the image of the opportunistic preacher, more concerned about the unholy trinity of sex, money, and power than the holy trinity, is vividly alive in the European perception of America. There is also a widespread impression that the new "electronic church" and the various evangelical movements that support it are questionable not just from a materialistic point of view, but also because of their tendency to preach "the gospel of success" rather than renunciation and suffering.

Harry appears to be a typical representative of a religious orientation that chooses the easy way out and runs away from any true confrontation with the difficulties of Christian doctrines. For him, religion is inextricable from sex and society. In Ruth's apartment, "the idea of making it while the churches are full excites him" (91), and the sight of Sunday dressed people walking to church seems to him "a visual proof of the unseen world" (91). His golf mate Eccles, whose situation is made more unbearable by the fact that he is a minister of the gospel, has "forgotten most of the theology they made him absorb" (161). He is shown to be utterly out of place in a Christian pulpit when he preaches a sermon on Christ's forty days in the Wilderness and His conversation with the Devil.

> Its larger significance, its greater meaning, Eccles takes to be this: suffering, deprivation, barrenness, hardship, lack are all an indispensable part of the education, the initiation, as it were, of any of those who would follow Jesus Christ. Eccles wrestles in the pulpit with the squeak in his voice. His eyebrows jiggle as if on fishhooks. It is an unpleasant and strained performance, contorted, somehow; he drives his car with an easier piety. In his robes he seems the sinister priest of a drab mystery. Harry has no taste for the dark, tangled, visceral aspect of Christianity, the *going through* quality of it, the passage *into* death and suffering that redeems and inverts these things, like an umbrella blowing inside out. He lacks the mindful will to walk the straight line of a paradox. His eyes turn toward the light however it glances into his retina. (237)

In Updike's view, the people who can walk the straight line of a paradox, thinkers like Søren Kierkegaard and Karl Barth, have perceived the true meaning of the challenge of the Christian vision. The affable social and psychological "engineering" of a man like Eccles is as inadequate a response to the mystery of religion as is Harry's instinctive turning toward the light in the line of least resistance. The true minister of the gospel in the novel, not incidentally speaking with a heavy German accent, is Fritz Kruppenbach, the minister of Mt. Judge's Lutheran church, "a man of brick," in Updike's phrase. Kruppenbach castigates Eccles for his lack of true belief, presenting to him a very different idea of the minister's role:

> When on Sunday morning then, when we go before their faces, we must walk up not worn out with misery but full of Christ, *hot*... with Christ, on *fire: burn* them with the force of our belief. That is why they come; why else would they pay us? Anything else we

> can do or say anyone can do or say. They have doctors and lawyers for that. (171)

Kruppenbach is out of place in Rabbit's world, a relic of an ancient past when Puritan ministers like Cotton Mather and Jonathan Edwards held sway in American pulpits. In *Rabbit, Run* the true preacher of the American gospel is Jimmy the Mouseketeer, with his message of how the development of our special talent is the way to be happy (10). Small wonder that the most memorable metaphor of the religious quest in the novel is a description of a game of golf! (168)[19]

It is hardly accidental that one of Harry's most important spiritual mentors in the novel is a figure from a Disney television show. Although the role of television in American life is not given much space in *Rabbit, Run,* except as an illustration of what Rabbit takes to be Janice's worthlessness, its presence and importance are much more significant than the surface impression suggests. Harry's frustration with Janice's television addiction is behind many of their quarrels, but Harry himself is only partly in opposition to the world of the tube. As Dilvo Ristoff has pointed out, he watches the screen for words of wisdom that he might apply to his professional and private life, and he even quotes Jimmy the Mouseketeer in one of his conversations with Eccles (107). Rabbit's feeble attempts at rebellion are all played out within the conventional culture of the Eisenhower fifties, when television for the first time became the dominant medium of communication and perception. "His disagreements with the establishment" appear "cosmetic rather than structural,"[20] and it should be no surprise to find Rabbit ten years later with an American flag stuck to his car or twenty years later reading hardly anything except *Consumer Reports.*

The brief sketch of his visit to the hospital where Janice gets her hour's worth of entertainment for a quarter, speaks volumes for American television culture:

> So for thirty minutes he sits by her bed watching some crew-cut M.C. tease a lot of elderly women from Akron, Ohio, and Oakland, California. The idea is all these women have tragedies they tell about and then get money according to how much applause there is, but by the time the M.C. gets done delivering commercials and kidding

> them about their grandchildren and their girlish hairdos there isn't much room for tragedy left. (217)

One might hope that Updike made this up, but the incredible tastelessness of a show of this kind would not be beyond the range of what a European might expect from the world of American junk TV.[21] For Updike's two protagonists, however, watching this show "even makes for a kind of peace; he and Janice hold hands" (217).

Janice is also the central character in Updike's presentation of the role played by alcohol in American middle-class culture, in the fifties and later. According to Betty Friedan, alcohol and tranquilizers are the American housewife's answer to what she calls "the problem that has no name."[22] Isolated from the world of seriously working America in the little nest her husband pays for and she is supposed to keep in order, the little woman is trying to pass her time. As Harry observes: "Well Jesus Janice. All you did was watch television and drink all the time" (215). The way alcohol permeates American culture, later joined more frequently and devastatingly by other drugs, is an important aspect of the image of America held by the average transatlantic observer. It is typical in such a culture that no one is quite sure who to blame when, at the end of the novel, Janice drowns her baby in a drunken stupor. When Harry cries out at the funeral, "You all keep acting as if *I* did it. I wasn't anywhere near. *She*'s the one" (296). For the others Harry's candor constitutes the elemental truth of *his* shockingly irresponsible behavior. Although Harry must obviously share the blame for baby Becky's tragic death, he does stand out as the only person in the novel who is trying to be a nondrinker (and nonsmoker). His athletic past, combined with his passion for neatness, order, and control, set him apart in this respect, and it is a measure of his decline that he is not strong enough to withstand the pressure of society's much messier ways.

When critics state that Updike is America's foremost chronicler of WASP (or almost-WASP) middle-class culture, they often fail to recognize that Updike, like many foreign observers, is acutely aware of the many layers of the middle class in America. One might not necessarily accept Paul Fussell's contention, in his witty and provocative *Class: A Guide Through the American Status System,* that there are nine classes in America,[23] but it is obvious that the abysmal separation between the rich and the poor will yield many different strata of income and life-style. In spite of many Americans' protestations to the contrary, Europeans are generally convinced that equality is less real in the United States than in most European nations. Even if the majority of Americans think of themselves as middle class, that concept is so inclusive and multilayered that the difference between top and bottom can be enormous. In *Rabbit, Run,* social distinctions (as well as the animosities they engender) are clearly visible. Mrs. Angstrom's hostility to Janice, for instance, seems to be largely based on her resentment of the Springers' too-easy rise to a higher social status than her own lower-middle-class position. When Janice has the thoughtless temerity, when she first appears in the Angstroms' humble home on Jackson Street, to ask why Mrs. Angstrom does not get a washing machine, the reaction is predictable: "All she meant was What was I doing living in such a run-down half-house when she came from a great big barn on Joseph Street with the kitchen full of gadgets" (159–60). Harry, on another occasion, observes that "the Springers were Episcopalians, more of the old phony's social climbing, they were originally Reformeds" (101). Evidently, even one's religious affiliation has a socioeconomic dimension in this kind of society.

In keeping with the importance played by cars in American society, it is also predictable that the males in *Rabbit, Run* define their social position in terms of the cars they drive. Reverend Eccles' desire to be popular and "with it" can be seen in his '58 olive Buick four-door, and the reader will easily believe that "he drives his car with an easier piety" (237) than he is able to evince in the pulpit. When Harry marries Janice, he moves up from a '36 Buick to a '55 Ford because his car-selling father-in-law is ashamed of having such an old, beat-up car in the family (26). One of the central ironies of the Rabbit novels is that Janice, the "moron" he is hitched to, is his passport upward in the social hierarchy. Mr. Springer, whose used-car lots have taken the family to their new position of affluence, may not be a very admirable person, but Rabbit's attitude, that "he's really kind of a jerk but a successful jerk at least" (227), testifies to the importance of money and success in Rabbit's America. No matter that this affluence is based on fraud and lies (217); in the American success story it is the amount of money that matters, not how it is earned.

The Americanness of *Rabbit, Run* from a transatlantic point of view seems focused in what Updike once in an interview referred to as the "yes, but" quality of his writing.[24] Updike's fiction consistently opens more doors than it closes and asks many more questions than there are simple answers to. In a novel like *Rabbit, Run,* the reader is continually invited to participate in a dialectic of different and sometimes contradictory viewpoints, where no one person or position can be identified as representing the truth. Harry Angstrom may not be capable of understanding his own struggle, but his creator never fails to trace the complexities of his various predicaments. Whether it is a question of freedom versus commitment, alienation versus belonging, faith versus skepticism, or egotism versus altruism, Updike manages to convey both the difficulty and the seriousness of the human condition. With what a cover blurb once called his "appalled affection" for Rabbit Angstrom, Updike has succeeded in giving us a protagonist who has scored anywhere from zero to nine on a scale of ten among the critics of the novel. This ambivalence, this insistence on continuing the open-minded quest for answers to the fundamental questions of human life, in society and in the universe, may ultimately be the most significant American tradition that *Rabbit, Run* upholds.

NOTES

1 *The American Myth and the European Mind: American Studies in Europe 1776–1960* (Philadelphia: University of Pennsylvania Press, 1961), p. 6.

2 For an interesting discussion of this phenomenon, see Pascal Privat, "Empire of the Fun," *Newsweek,* April 13, 1992: 10–19.

3 This anecdote is recounted in Roger Rollin, ed., *The Americanization of the Global Village: Essays in Comparative Popular Culture* (Bowling Green, Ohio: Bowling Green State University Popular Press, 1989), p. 2.

4 For information on foreign translations of Updike's work, I am indebted to Elizabeth A. Gearhart, *John Updike: A Comprehensive Bibli-*

ography with Selected Annotations (Darby, PA: Norwood Editions, 1980), pp. 10–16.

5 The extent to which *Rabbit, Run* might be seen to illustrate central characteristics of "the Me Decade" of the 1970s is quite striking. See, for instance, Christopher Lasch, *The Culture of Narcissism: American Life in an Age of Diminishing Expectations* (New York: Norton, 1979), one of the best known studies of American culture to appear in Europe in recent years.

6 "Why Rabbit Had to Go," *The New York Times Book Review* (5 August 1990): 24.

7 One should perhaps note here that the European perception of "the American mind" is still to a large extent based on a dominant WASP middle-class ideology. And until the "political correctness" debate reaches Hollywood, this situation is not likely to change.

8 Besides being an obvious reference to the theme of existential anxiety in the novel, Angstrom is the Americanized version of a common Swedish surname.

9 *Rabbit, Run* (New York: Alfred A. Knopf, 1960, rev. and rpt. 1970). Subsequent references to this edition of the novel will appear parenthetically in the text.

10 Both Tothero and Eccles make fun of Rabbit's job (52, 102), and Harry himself observes that "I don't suppose you're supposed to like your job. If you did, then it wouldn't be a job" (221). This echoes Updike's statement in an interview: "My novels are all about the search for useful work. So many people these days have to sell things they don't believe in and have jobs that defy describing." Quoted by Judie Newman, *John Updike* (London: Macmillan, 1988), p. 33.

11 For a comprehensive discussion of the role of women in the 1950s, see Betty Friedan, *The Feminine Mystique* (Harmondsworth, England: Penguin Press, 1963).

12 Joseph Waldmeir, in his analysis of Rabbit's quest, calls Harry an "intuitive essentialist," but goes on to say that his transcendental quest "is so unearthly as to be incapable of articulation or even of attainment." See his "It's the Going That's Important, Not the Getting There: Rabbit's Questing Non-Quest," *Modern Fiction Studies* 37 (Spring 1991): 18.

13 "Self-Reliance," rpt. in *Emerson's Essays: First and Second Series* (New York: E.P. Dutton, 1906), p. 31.

14 Updike himself has referred to "an America where, for most of us, there seems little to do but to feel." See *Assorted Prose* (New York: Alfred A. Knopf, 1965), p. 235.

15 For an excellent discussion of this "scene-oriented" and historically conditioned aspect of Updike's work, see Dilvo I. Ristoff, *Updike's America: The Presence of Contemporary History in John Updike's Rabbit Trilogy* (New York: Peter Lang, 1988), esp. pp. 39–73.

16 It is interesting to note here that Updike at one point thought of subtitling the novel "A Movie," and that he has put a great deal of emphasis on the importance of the novel's use of present tense to express the immediacy of the moment. See "Why Rabbit Had to Go," 1.

17 Clinton Burhans, Jr. stresses the oedipal sources of Harry's inability to mature and realize a satisfactory relationship with Janice. See "Things Falling Apart: Structure and Theme in *Rabbit, Run,*" *Modern Fiction Studies* 37 (Spring 1991): 18.

18 It will also seem strange to most European ears to hear Mr. Springer address his twenty-two-year-old daughter as "darling" and "baby" on the phone (238).

19 Derek Wright, in an excellent article on *Rabbit, Run,* has noted how Updike materializes religion and sacralizes sex and sports in the novel, thus obscuring the fundamental difference between the transcendent and the immanent physical levels of existence. Thus Rabbit's quest for that "something that wants me to find it" becomes even more confused and self-defeating. See "Mapless Motion: Form and Space in Updike's *Rabbit, Run,*" *Modern Fiction Studies* 37 (Spring 1991): 43.

20 *Updike's America,* p. 73.

21 The appearance of American-style game shows on European television channels in recent years has, even more than soap operas, polarized the audience into scoffers and enthusiasts, with the latter in a predictable majority for the more popular shows like "Wheel of Fortune" and "The Dating Game." This divided response to the "Americanization" of Europe is further illustrated by the controversy over Euro-Disney outside of Paris, called by one critic "a cultural Chernobyl."

22 *The Feminine Mystique,* pp. 13–29.

23 (New York: Summit Books, 1983), p. 27. The classes Fussell designates are: Top out-of-sight, Upper, Upper middle, Middle, High proletarian, Mid-proletarian, Low proletarian, Destitute, Bottom out-of-sight.

24 For an interesting discussion of this dialectical quality of Updike's art, see George W. Hunt, *John Updike and the Three Great Secret Things: Sex, Religion, and Art* (Grand Rapids, MI: William B. Eerdmans Publishing Co., 1980), pp. 20–1.

5

"Unadorned Woman, Beauty's Home Image": Updike's *Rabbit, Run*

STACEY OLSTER

> Let me, testing the thin ice, begin as far back in time as my memory can reach, with my maternal grandmother.... I still remember the strain on her sharp-nosed face as she stared upward at me while I crouched on a lower branch of a tree. That was one of the things women did, I early concluded: they tried to get you to come down out of a tree. She was afraid I would fall, and that possibility had occurred to me also, so I was half grateful to be called down. But the other half, it seemed, needed to climb higher and higher, in defiance of the danger.
>
> –John Updike, "Women," *Odd Jobs: Essays and Criticism*

"AMERICAN fiction is notoriously thin on women," John Updike once remarked when asked about how much he sees himself as belonging to an American literary tradition. Asserting "I *have* attempted a number of portraits of women," and contrasting his own inclusions with the notable omissions of nineteenth-century male novelists, he ended by speculating, "we may have reached that point of civilization, or decadence, where we *can* look at women. I'm not sure Mark Twain *was* able to."[1] There is looking, of course – and then there is looking. Harry Angstrom has no difficulty looking at women in *Rabbit, Run* – his gazing at wives and waifs, strangers and sisters, mothers and matrons makes him a consummate voyeur. So able is he to look at women that he even starts looking for them in inanimate objects. "In his head he is talking to the clubs as if they're women," Updike writes, describing Harry on the golf course. "The irons, light and thin yet somehow treacherous in his hands, are Janice.... with the woods the 'she' is Ruth," and when "she" betrays him with a shot that goes off into the grass, "the bush is damn somebody, his mother."[2]

A Freudian field day, to be sure, portraying the female as meant to shelter ("Home is the hole" [132]) and the male as meant to reign supreme (the [golf] ball is a "hard irreducible pellet that is not really himself yet in a way is; just the way it sits there in the center of everything" [132]), the passage vindicates the kind of sports therapy that Reverend Eccles undertakes with Harry, based on his diagnosis that "the thing that makes Harry unsteady, that makes him unable to repeat his beautiful effortless swing every time, is the thing at the root of all the problems that he has created" (168). The passage also suggests the root of many of the problems Updike has created for himself with women, particularly with feminist critics who find more to object to in his work than the objectification of women as everything from sports equipment to foliage. Updike conceives of golf as the game "wherein the wall between us and the supernatural is rubbed thinnest." The mystical "it" that a well placed ball can bring (134), what Updike later will specify as "the hope of perfection, of a perfect weightlessness and consummate ease, . . . grace you could call it," is seen as conferring on men the right to transcendent flight, and to condemn women, for all their succoring, to a life of constantly being flown over, a view displayed in all Updike's subsequent fiction.[3]

For most of the critics who cavil against Updike's treatment of women, it is not simply that he portrays his women characters as physically flawed (Mary Gordon's contention), as intellectually limited (Mary Allen's hobbyhorse), as closest to mutts and monkeys.[4] Nor is it only that they are seen as imprisoning men within "a sophisticated Oedipal knot," as Josephine Hendin proposes, so that "getting into a woman means getting back to their mothers' kitchens where there is guilt and frustration for them and hate for any woman who threatens to melt the iced anger that binds them to their mothers."[5] Because Updike subscribes to the notion that "[p]lain realism has never seemed to me enough,"[6] the social and psychological attributes granted to women in his works have spiritual and archetypal reverberations. And it is in fitting women into the dualist metaphysical scenarios that form the plots of his novels, whether as Earth Mothers or Venuses, mainly as of "a different race" (93), that Updike draws the greatest ire, for in doing so he is presumed to imply, as his most intentionally mythological work states, "[t]heir value is not present to themselves, but is given to them by men."[7]

Critics more sympathetic to Updike's designs have tried to exert a degree of damage control in locating a shift in his subsequent novels toward a reconciliation of opposites. Thus, having cited Updike's democratic projection of Venus onto nearly every female character and having centered "*the* nuclear fable" of his life around "the Mother who waits out in Nature," or "Venus in her older, wiser, and more terrifying form," Joyce Carol Oates sees the marriage that ends *Couples* as a breakthrough for Updike, breaking down the divisions between real and ideal love that have characterized Piet Hanema's relations with the opposite sex up to that point. Tracing this confusion of characteristics to a later novel, *The Witches of Eastwick*, Kathleen Verduin sees Updike's endowing women with attributes that usually define his men – notably, fear of death – as evidence of his "struggling to come to terms with his own tendency toward dualism" in a novel that displays "an honest effort to revaluate a similar dualism, the polarization of the sexes."[8] I would add Updike's more recent portrait of S. deserting husband and home for the freedom of an Arizona ashram as not only reworking a nineteenth-century novel of another author, *The Scarlet Letter*, but as revamping with respect to gender a twentieth-century novel of his own, *Rabbit, Run*. Reviewing that prototypical Updike novel of a man fleeing the nets of domesticity and death from the perspective of his later works shows that revamping need not imply reversal of his earlier treatment of women. His second novel contains the seeds of subsequent emendations. In the difference between the cad and the chronicler, even a cad whom Updike has admitted is "not essentially advanced" over himself,[9] is the difference between the inarticulate literalist for whom, whatever his far-reaching longings, words mean what they say, and the literary imagist for whom language can juxtapose exposition and exposé. More to the point, in the juxtaposition of the voices of the men and women in *Rabbit, Run*, Updike questions whether the impulse toward sexual mythologizing is limited to one character, or one author, or bespeaks instead a need to seek in an archetypal Other "a glorious message from the deep" that typifies every human being, regardless of gender.[10]

Any evaluation of Updike's treatment of women must include (even at the risk of repeating a commonplace) some discussion of "More Love in the Western World," the essay in which he addresses Denis de Rougemont's contentions that " 'the inescapable conflict in the West between passion and marriage' " lies in a split between the realms of spirit and matter, and that love becomes "not a way of accepting and entering the world but a way of defying and escaping it."[11] Directed toward an "Unattainable Lady" who, in her idealized state, embodies " 'the very essence of what is strange in woman,' " yet presents the inherently egocentric lover a crystallization of his past and herself as "alpha and omega, as his Fate,"[12] love in the Western world so confirms the lover in his own sense of importance that the prospects of such an estimable self being extinguished diminish to nought. As Updike explains, "Our fundamental anxiety is that we do not exist – or will cease to exist. Only in being loved do we find external corroboration of the supremely high valuation each ego secretly assigns itself."[13] Simply put, a "man in love ceases to fear death."[14] The caveat is that this most tantalizing of loves must remain the most tremendous of teases; once transferred to the realm of the real, with a woman whose physical imperfections – not to mention mortality – are as certain as those of the lover, the ability of this Doreen Gray to minister to the lover's need vanishes for what she reveals is exactly what he does not want to see. " '[T]o possess her,' " as de Rougemont recognized, " 'is to lose her.' "[15] To remain with her is even worse, for mired in her own earthbound condition, she cannot help but drag the lover down as well.

D. H. Lawrence provided perhaps the most literal depiction of that danger in the two drowned bodies dredged from the lake in *Women in Love*, the woman's arms wrapped around the neck of the man in a strangling embrace. Updike comes a close second in the demise he sketches for the grandfather in "The Blessed Man of Boston, My Grandmother's Thimble, and Fanning Island": Trying to jump from a bed he thinks is on fire, he is restrained by the "disproportionate strength" of his sickly wife who "clung to him and in their fall to the floor he died."[16] But, raised in Berks County, Pennsylvania, and not Boston, as a Lutheran not a Calvinist, Updike does not fully inherit the Manichean legacy to which de Rougemont directly traced the "modern Occidental obsession with romantic love."[17] Updike's admiration of Hawthorne for having written "the one classic from the lusty youth of American literature that deals with society in its actual heterosexual weave"[18] is tempered by his awareness of the morally conflicted stances in which Hawthorne's "instinctive tenet that matter and spirit are inevitably at war" ("Earth-flesh-blood versus Heaven-mind-spirit") eventuated: an attraction to sensual women that mars the promotion of their ethereal sisters as models of virtue, a rejoicing in the fall of a Dimmesdale as it represents the demise of the Puritan heritage he embodies.[19]

In populating the landscape of *Rabbit, Run* with women who conform to no one (or, more to the point, two) physical type(s), Updike complicates the dualist portrayals of earlier American heroines, just as his tale of Rabbit moving among them, a Lawrencian "son of the morning" (151), complicates the connotations of the choices made by earlier American heroes. This is reflected in the very beginning of the Rabbit tetralogy. When Harry Angstrom opts to leave his wife, in whose overflowing ashtrays he sees a Slough of Despond and whose thinning hair signals an irreversible movement "only going one way, toward deeper wrinkles and skimpier hair" (11), he grants himself honorary membership in the Kiwanis Club of American male characters defined by Leslie Fiedler (in the same year of *Rabbit, Run*'s publication) as fearing "the fall to sex, marriage, and responsibility" that any confrontation between man and woman brings, with all the intimations of mortality that the word "fall" connotes.[20] Yet making his pilgrim's progress from the fat and totally real Janice (as confirmed by her pregnancy) to the fleshy and tempting promise of Ruth (Venus as confirmed by her past promiscuity) provides Rabbit with little relief. The weightiness he resents about Janice's pregnancy is a burden Harry literally carries with him throughout the novel, crippling his basketball playing in the book's first pages, forcing him to see himself an "old man" out of place among "boys" (6, 3), and in *Rabbit at Rest* ballooning into a two-hundred-thirty-pound paunch that leaves him "big-bellied" with a "vague doom" he tries to repress (46). The death's head that peeps through Janice's thinning hair reappears in Marty Tothero's patchy tufts (42) and Jack Eccles's "small-jawed head [showing] its teeth like a skull" (121). Ronnie Harrison's "[f]at and half bald" appearance so oppresses Rabbit that he becomes "obsessed by Harrison's imperfections" (175). Rabbit's car is a "stiff shroud" smaller than his apartment (40); Tothero's Sunshine Athletic Association room is devoid of even a closet whose door Harry must open only halfway lest it hit a television set. Ejecting himself from the claustrophobia of living with Janice (emotionally equivalent to being "in your coffin before they've taken your blood out" [215–16]) only projects Harry into the greater claustrophobia of the coffin-like spaces he inhabits without her. With the world of decay Harry has embodied in Janice superseded by signs of decrepitude in the masses, Updike exposes from the start how erroneous is Harry's propensity to limit the threat to one woman or even one gender.

Tothero, Eccles, and Harrison do not sleep with Harry, however (although homoerotic overtures from the first two do cause him discomfort). It is in the sexual relations between men and women that Updike situates the transcendental gamble against death most intensely, sex functioning for so many of his characters "as the emergent religion, as the only thing left."[21] Introduced as the physical opposite of Janice, thick-haired and "pleasingly dexterous" (64), Ruth Leonard appears to be just what the dualist metaphysical doctor ordered. With her large body portrayed in terms of spatial expansiveness, "an incredible continent" (81), she actualizes in the flesh "the broad soft belly of the land" Harry has sought to penetrate on his abortive flight from home (30). When christened "Mrs. America" (70), she even awakens memories of that native land whose piercing historians like Frederick Jackson Turner had lauded at the turn of the century. Unlike Vera Hummel in *The Centaur,* whose deification as "goddess-size" by the Caldwell males is corroborated by a mythic underpinning that enables a physical education instructor to play Venus in gym shorts with no difficulty,[22] Ruth needs something of a makeover before assuming the role Harry assigns her in Updike's more realistic novel. Only when scrubbed of make-up and stripped of diaphragm at Harry's command can her "frozen form" assume the appropriate "pose" Harry desires (82), that of "perfect statue," in the words of the novel's first edition, "unadorned woman, beauty's home image," thus anticipating the women made objects for gazing that populate Updike's later works: the life-size nude encased in bronze in *The Centaur*'s museum; Peggy, in *Of the Farm*, who models sporadically; the wife in "Museums and Women" who is as "fair, and finely formed, and mute" as an eighteenth-century statuette, the mistress whose head and shoulders form a bust before a tapestry; most of the women in *Couples* (Angela, who poses "like Eve on a portal," Marcia, who reminds her lover of a Greek statue, even the Transparent Woman in the planetarium, who makes the Hanema girls think of their mother).[23] The question that must be asked, however, is whose "home image" is she?

Updike has made no secret of his propensity to think of women's bodies in mythologized terms. "The female body is, in its ability to conceive and carry a fetus and to nurse an infant, our life's vehicle," he recently wrote. "Male sexuality, then, returning to this primal source, drinks at the spring of being and enters the murky region, where up is down and death is life, of mythology."[24] So, too, does he attribute specific spiritual connotations to specific sexual acts. "Fellatio, buggery – the sexual specifics are important," he stated when discussing the "lifelong journey into the bodies of women" that is advanced over the four Rabbit novels, "for they mark the stages of a kind of somatic pilgrimage that, smile though we will, is consciously logged by most men and perhaps by more women than admit it."[25] Much of this contemporary mythologizing of women is not unique to Updike. Thomas Pynchon's query, "What sort of mistress, then, would Venus be?" underlies the entirety of *V.*, in which mortal versions of the title character become increasingly inanimate, pass through a brief incarnation in a Botticelli painting, and culminate in a chapter that conflates a goddess of sexual love, Astarte; the Maltese word for "woman," Mara; a city of feminine gender, Valletta; and a peninsula in which they all reside that is shaped like the mons Veneris. Norman Mailer's assumption that women "were a step, or a stage, or a move or a leap nearer the creation of existence" than men and hence men's "indispensable and only connection to the future," and his ascribing to the womb an "unaccountable liaison with the beyond," explain his invoking "Sex as Time, and Time as the connection of new circuits" at the end of *The Deer Park*, his proposing the moment of a woman's first orgasm as "The Time of Her Time" in a short story, and his taking Rabbit's contraceptive demand one step further in *An American Dream* by having Stephen Rojack remove a woman's diaphragm himself in the middle of lovemaking.[26]

Refuting the feminist charge that such biological mythologizing of Woman in the abstract occurs at the expense of women portrayed in fiction as all-too-real, Updike remains fully aware of the dangers of sacrificing what Joanne Dobson has called the "*fact* of woman" to the "*idea* of woman." He writes, "The largeness of our mother-myth has a paradoxically dwindling effect upon the women concerned: they must be in all things motherly and become therefore natural processes rather than people."[27] Accusers view very different male authors perpetrating (and perpetuating) very similar American literary crimes: Mary Gordon lambastes Updike for extending in Rabbit the "pattern of moving boys killing females who get in their way." Judith Fetterley upbraids Mailer for dictating that women "must be killed and killed violently and thoroughly and again and again before the hero is able to break free and head for the West." Comparisons between these two worst offenders, however, show Updike questioning the tendency to mythologize as he delineates the reasons characters continue to portray each other in mythologized terms.[28]

For Mailer, who premises his metaphysics on God being at war with the Devil and every conflict on earth reverberating in that overarching cosmological struggle, the battle he projects onto the bodies of women has ramifications with respect to the ascendancy of creation or decreation. Within this largest of schemata, in which each person is assigned a particular mission, "one of us to create, another to be brave, a third to love, a fourth to work, a fifth to be bold, a sixth to be all of these,"[29] man's venture into the sexual arena demands more than "the adventurous juncture of ego and courage" that confrontation with those who "possess the better half of life already" might entail.[30] It constitutes, quite simply, "the mirror of how we approach God through our imperfections."[31] To the degree that sex advances the cause of God's creation – creation in the most literal sense – the sexual specifics in Mailer's work gain meaning: The difference between anal and vaginal sex is thus denoted as "a raid on the Devil and a trip back to the Lord." For all the rhapsodizing Stephen Rojack does when describing the first orgasm in which "I came up from my body rather than down from my mind...and the honey she had given me I could only give back, all sweets to her womb, all come in her cunt," the pleasure he and Cherry experience is less important than the pregnancy in which their act culminates.[32] The Lord, Mailer averred, "was not thus devoted to the absurd as to put the orgasm in the midst of the act of creation without cause of the profoundest sort, for when a man and woman conceive, would it not be best that they be able to see one another for a transcendent instant, as if the soul of what would then be conceived might live with more light later?"[33]

For Updike, who has no doubts about God's omnipotence and openly prefers "a fierce God above the kind God" who is "the more or less watered-down Puritan God" that most people now worship,[34] there is no need to invest human beings, much less human sexuality, with the larger sense of mission that Mailer ascribes to them. He who delivers the message that "God gives to each one of us a special talent" in *Rabbit, Run* is a grown man who prances around on television in mouse ears (9). Moreover, the exact processes that signal creation for Mailer signal corrosion for Updike. Harry regains "his old inkling" that "there was something that wanted him to find it, that he was here on earth on a kind of assignment" after experiencing anal sex in *Rabbit is Rich* as "a void, a pure black box, a casket of perfect nothingness."[35] But the procreation that results from genital sex offers little that is any more promising, for in a world in which "[t]hings compete; a life demands a life,"[36] in which, as the opening to *Rabbit, Run* asserts, "the kids keep coming, they keep crowding you up" (3), the birth of the child confirms the death of the parent. "The fullness ends when we give Nature her ransom, when we make children for her," Harry realizes when he looks at the two-year-old Nelson. "Then she is through with us, and we become, first inside, and then outside, junk" (226). Having this early recognized his hierarchical place within "the vertical order of parenthood" Updike proposes (308), Harry remains antagonistic toward the adult Nelson for having "swallowed up the boy that was and substituted one more pushy man in the world,"[37] relenting only when Nelson's own paternity establishes him as a "hostage he's given to fortune,"

Nelson's thinning hair reminding Harry that "[y]our children's losing battle with time seems even sadder than your own."[38]

What Harry does not realize, until it is too late, is that Nature does not wait to make its point until the pitter patter of little feet has become audible. The same statement about Nature's opportunistic manners appears after Ruth and Rabbit have completed their first act of lovemaking: "Nature leads you up like a mother and as soon as she gets her little price leaves you with nothing" (86). That such a statement appears after the moment of orgasm, an experience Ruth has forgotten she could have, is revealing since it is as "nothing" that Updike portrays that moment of physical sensation. This reflects the attitude of Updike's main protagonist in *Rabbit, Run.* "Yesterday morning the sky was ribbed with thin-stretched dawn clouds, and he was exhausted, heading into the center of the net, where alone there seemed a chance of rest," Harry recalls, comparing the time before he met Ruth to the time after he has slept with her. "Now the noon of another day has burned away the clouds, and the sky in the windshield is blank and cold, and he feels nothing ahead of him, Ruth's blue-eyed nothing, the nothing she told him she did" (97).

This "nothing" by which Ruth is defined refers, in its most literal sense, to an anatomical absence, the same absence Peter Caldwell discovers when pressing his face against Penny's skirt in *The Centaur* ("where her legs meet there is nothing") and in which he then locates "the secret the world holds at its center."[39] In *Rabbit, Run,* however, this "nothing" also denotes both Ruth's absence of regular employment and the fact that what she does for a living is take money for sexual favors. In fact, in the social world of the novel, money serves as the common denominator of all the women in whose sexuality Harry seeks relief from the base materiality of his daily life, from the whore who takes him into her room in Texas ("Sweet woman, *she* was money" [47]); to Janice, whose father owns Springer Motors; to Ruth, whom he prices at ten cents a pound (72); to, most of all, the Du Pont woman he envisions barefoot beside a swimming pool in France and who symbolizes to Harry the greatest escape of all: "Something like money in a naked woman, deep, millions" (26). More important, within the religious dimension that Updike's works typically seek, money increasingly becomes used by the characters as an index of spirituality. In the most Americanist of senses, the foreclosure of Kroll's department store that had stood "bigger than a church" comes to signify to Harry the forfeiture of divine election: "When the money stopped, they could close down God Himself."[40] With woman now functioning as the place where the spiritual and the sexual meet, no wonder Harry will begin connecting woman as blank with woman as bank: "A blank check. A woman is blank until you fuck her."[41] Therefore, blankness is the condition Harry strives to maintain in women, having already established the "vast blank of his freedom" as a polar – and temporal – opposite to all that stinks of the grave that he has embodied in Janice and their shared apartment (51). He thus loves the fact that Ruth dismisses five former suitors who telephone her at home, for in cutting herself off from her past she encases herself in a perpetual present: "the past was a vine hanging on by just these five tendrils and it tore away easily, leaving her clean and blue and blank" (173). He delights in watching her swim and treasures how "[c]lean, clean" she looks when in water, for in water her body refuses to sink but keeps floating to the surface of its own buoyancy (142).

Harry's body displays no such buoyancy, though, for it is a leaden inability to sustain an erection that characterizes him as a lover: "it is here he most often failed Janice, by coming too soon" (85). And, as the fate of baby Becky dramatically testifies, bodies in water can only stay afloat for so long. In other words, Harry's desire to endow sex with transcendent properties and envision women as goddesses impervious to time is offset by the denouement Updike attaches to sexual activity that depicts lovemaking between men and women as a temporally bound process. Harry traces that change to his getting married, Janice's orgasms "never as good on their own" bed as they were on the bed borrowed from a friend (41). But since Harry only marries Janice because she gets pregnant, he places the blame on pregnancy for the change in women's sexual potential, when flesh becomes flab, when the "wonderful way they have of coming forward around you when they want it" turns to "just fat weight" (26) – and pregnancy not just for the physical threat of childbirth exposing women to mortal harm. Harry "loves women when they're first pregnant" (307), and Updike (no Hemingway in this regard) typically portrays difficult periods of labor in order to highlight the successful deliveries in which they end.[42] But women's pregnancy for Harry later becomes "stubborn lumpiness" when the man who seeks "to bury himself in her" (10, 307) is displaced by a fetus whose destruction of lap prefigures its later displacement of its father. No longer a provider of comfort against fears of death, carrying, indeed nurturing, proof of Harry's inescapable doom inside her body, a pregnant woman to Harry comes to lose all value, and his portrait of her shifts from terms of money to terms of metal: Janice after Becky's birth is a "machine, a white, pliant machine for fucking, hatching, feeding" (234). Unable to grant her even the power of Henry Adams' dynamo, Harry reduces this fallen Virgin to the status of the gadgets he sells, knowing full well, as he will later say of the used gadgets he sells at her father's car lot, that "Metal corrodes."[43]

What Harry experiences as infuriating change, Updike understands as inevitable continuity, a difference encapsulated in the contrast between Harry's experience of Mrs. Smith's garden and Updike's portrayal of it.[44] Filled with trees Harry associates with "forbidden estates" (139), the garden surpasses that most forbidden of biblical estates to be "like Heaven" for him (223); yet the immunity from time it promises Harry (signified by his never having to cut his fingernails while working there) is undercut by the testament to time's passage that the portraits inside Mrs. Smith's house display: the disparity between the young woman whose "short puffy little upper lip" looks "so good in a girl" (222) and the gnarled widow in whom Harry finds her incarnated. Viewed within the antipastoral terms in which Updike works, in which the recomposition of plants through photosynthesis and the decomposition of glucose through human respiration are opposing processes,[45] and which, in *Rabbit, Run,* culminate with Rebecca June Angstrom's death in the spring month for which she is named, Rabbit's mythologizing of women as creatures of nature is misdirected from the start.[46] This is particularly the case with his pursuit of the woman who lives on Summer Street. And predicating Ruth's ideality on her purity, cleansing her face of artificial "crust" and coverings (82), and freeing their act from any contraceptive plastics so he can enter her "split pod, an open fold, shapeless and simple" and stretch time "to great length and thinness" (84) prove moot given the way that Updike introduces Harry's amorous approach: "He makes love to her as he would to his wife" (83). Likewise, the very emblems Harry takes as proof that "the world just can't touch you" (109) Updike treats as tokens of his earthbound vulnerability: the orgasm he enables Ruth to have portrayed as "falling through" (86), an image of descent that prefigures the threat of Skylab falling in *Rabbit Is Rich* and the airplane crashes in *Rabbit at Rest,* all of which signal mortality; the godlike pride he feels at having "made you [Ruth] and the sun and the stars" betrayed by the words with which he appraises his final product, "naked in the shower, her hair hanging oozy with lather, her neck bowed to the whipping water," a Venus de Milo with arms: "I made you bloom" (109).

Even the domination over her to which Harry feels entitled is shown by Updike to be predicated on false premises when being "her master . . . [and] getting on top of her" are rights Harry assumes are his "by nature" (304). Indeed, the moment Harry takes as evidence of his greatest mastery, when he literally gets most "on top of her" having forced Ruth onto her knees in submission, the moment he initiates as a final closing on his property seeing the act she performs as "prov[ing] you're mine," thus confirming once and for all his noncorporeal status in that he stands before her like "an angel waiting for a word" (187), is the exact moment that Updike's images merge together to establish Harry's own corporeality in that he is the only one capable of coming into time with the act of fellatio he forces Ruth to perform. It becomes quite fitting, during this last visit, that his final assertion "of being by nature her master, of getting on top of her" plunges him back into the very world from which he has sought Ruth's body as refuge: "His hands and legs are suffused with a paralyzing sense of reality; his child is really dead, his day is really done" (304). As he learns later with respect to another kind of possession, "to be rich is to be robbed, to be rich is to be poor."[47]

To a certain extent, Harry does sense Updike's point – that sexuality ends not in resurrection, but in rot. His memory of making love with Janice on her girlfriend's bed is pierced by a recollection of "feeling lost, having done the final thing" (14). The dream he has after first making love to Ruth, which is populated by the women in his family, is permeated by images of metal and "tin-smelling coldness" (88). The icebox, "mottled with the same disease the linoleum has" (88), becomes, in the dream's associative logic, the Pandora's box that causes Janice's skin to slide off her face; it springs from Tothero's earlier description of his wife's skin as clumsily stitched together (54), but it also suggests the particular skin disease of psoriasis that Updike and his autobiographical surrogate Peter Caldwell inherit from their mothers and that a friend of Peter's directly links with sexuality in questioning whether it is syphilis.[48] Yet the dream that instills doubts in Rabbit about the role in which he has cast one woman in particular, indicated when he sees Ruth's "bush a froth of tinted metal" upon awakening (89), engenders no doubts about his mythologizing of women in general. Having "become domestic" with Ruth so quickly (90), he begins looking for a replacement of more refinement. When he meets Lucy Eccles, he immediately casts her as a "fine-grained Ruth" (118), mythologizes her legs spread as "two white gates parted" (232), and invests their relationship (such as it is) with the same qualities of property and ownership with which he previously defined that between himself and her predecessor: "He knows only this: underneath everything, under their minds and their situations, he possesses, like an inherited lien on a distant piece of land, a dominance over her, and that in her grain, in the lie of her hair and nerves and fine veins, she is prepared for this dominance" (240). When the door that Lucy eventually slams in his face indicates he cannot claim these rights, he transfers his sexual impulse, a wish "like a small angel" (243), to a different woman – Janice again – in whose "fullness that calls to him" he starts to envision the fleshiness of others, in whose bent form he sees a body ripe to proclaim as *"Mine, my woman,"* but whose "smeared frantic face" promptly "blots out his pride of possession" (285).

In contrast to the male characters in the works of an author like Mailer, who divide up women by type – fiery Latin brunettes, Marilyn Monroe blondes, Margot Macomber killers – and personify various national traits in those physical aspects, Updike's Rabbit is an absolute egalitarian in that any fertile woman provides grounds (pun intended) for deification. His rotations foreshadow the ongoing square dance that will characterize wife swapping in *Couples*. As a result, Janice is correct and her terminology particularly appropriate when she complains that Harry uses her only as "a pot for his dirt" (251). The resilience Harry continues to display in his pursuit of women may prove to some, as it does to Mrs. Smith, that Harry has the gift of "life" (224), but Updike undermines his efforts at every turn, proving more conclusively that Harry's mythologizing impulses just keep him going around and around in circles that get smaller and smaller as time goes on, and Harry begins revisiting the sites of former failures. If his first pursuit of Janice can be described as nostalgic, an effort by Harry to keep her a girl, "still scarcely adult," even presexually timeless in that her breasts, when flattened against her chest, revert to "tipped softness" (11), his final attempt to make her body keeper of "this little flame" he brings from church is nothing less than desperate (271).

And the women – far from "dumb bovine" creatures whose lack of education Mary Allen equates with a lack of intelligence – recognize the inevitable failure to which mythologizing impulses are doomed. Realizing that for Rabbit "it is not her body he wants, not the machine, but her, her" (79), Ruth recalls how often sex with others was similarly a question of mind over matter. "They couldn't have felt much it must have been just the *idea* of you" (147), she thinks when comparing Harry to the boys she dated in high school and judging as adolescent the quality of Harry's quest. Aware as well of the misogynistic impulse that turning women into "something pasted on the inside of their dirty heads" may reflect (146), suspecting, as the novel's first edition states, "[i]t was like they hated women and used *her*" (123), she fully recognizes what Harry's urge "to crush her" and his need "for pressure, just pure pressure" indicate: "Kill felt more like it," she replies to his pitiful excuse of having given her a "hug" (75, 76). Even Janice, who lacks the vocabulary as well as the experience of Ruth, still knows enough to view with skepticism all attempts to turn sex into a transcendent experience. "What did he and God talk about," Janice wonders after Harry returns from church in a state of arousal, "thinking," like all men, "about whatever they do think about" whenever they need to "[get] rid of this little hot clot that's bothering them" (251).

True, these women indulge in a certain degree of generalizing, if not mythologizing, themselves, as their questioning of men's motives indicates. Ruth's Joycean monologue ends much the same as Molly Bloom's does, with all her previous men conflated into one particular man, as she "forgave them all then, his face all their faces gathered into a scared blur" (148). The difference is that any such mythologizing for Updike's women springs less from sexual difference than from sexual precocity and sputters out in simple boredom: "If they'd just thought, they might have known you were curious too, that you could like that strangeness there like they liked yours, no worse than women in their way, all red wrinkles, my God, what was it in the end? No mystery. That was the great thing she discovered, that it was no mystery, just a stuck-on-looking bit that made them king" (146). Furthermore, unlike Molly Bloom, who comes to a similar conclusion about man's body, his genitals "two bags full and his other thing hanging down out of him or sticking up at you like a hatrack no wonder they hide it with a cabbageleaf," but continues to mythologize woman's body as "beauty of course thats admitted,"[49] the women in *Rabbit, Run* view their own bodies mainly as vehicles for social security. Sex for Ruth is work, with oral sex "just harder work" (146). Like any form of labor, it serves as a means for her to establish a particular social position, as her memories of having obliged high school boys indicate: "if you went along with it could be good or not so good and anyway put you with them against those others, those little snips running around her at hockey in gym. . . . But she got it back at night, taking what they didn't know existed like a queen" (146–7). Significantly, "queen" is the very title Harry confers on her after they first sleep together (113). Coming from a family with more money and therefore some social position to begin with, Janice sees sex as providing her with a way of acquiring a different kind of role: "She would be a woman with a house on her own" (250). For both, the antagonists they battle are not men, but women – the high school "girls with their contractors and druggists for fathers" who surround Ruth (147), the mother who humiliates Janice into a state of total inferiority. Thus, whereas women prove essential to men's scenarios, men prove auxiliary to theirs. In Updike's world, women are as much at war with each other as they are with men. More often than not, men who complain about women's dumbness get their ideas from their mothers since the mythology piercing in which younger women indulge threatens the one myth that justifies the power that being "still attached to the cord of his life" enables a mother to wield over her son, making men like Harry feel "they're not even in a way separate people he began in her stomach and if she gave him life she can take it away and if he feels that withdrawal it will be the grave itself" (289).[50]

In the end, neither Ruth nor Janice retains any illusions as to the extended benefits sex can provide. Janice realizes that, after marriage, she still remains "little clumsy dark-complected Janice Springer" (252). Ruth recognizes, as the television show watched by Harry proclaims, that one can be "Queen For A Day" and only a day; having been the victim when younger of locker room talk that refuted any hope of social position, Ruth as an adult looks at sex as a very limited enterprise: "You make love, you try to get close to somebody" (186). Since Updike's book is set in 1959, these thoughts are more appropriate for women than the mythologizing in which Harry, whose later intellectual life will consist of reading *Consumer Reports* on can openers, indulges. To question, as Mary Allen does, "what about work for women?" is to ask the wrong question of a novel set in a period of time in which 34,374,000 out of a noninstitutional population of 117,881,000 defined their role as "keeping house," in which 38,053,000 (or 62.8 percent) of a total of 60,569,000 women did not belong to the labor force, and in which day care for those, like Janice, with small children and few financial resources was not an available option, as indicated by the fact that of the 12,205,000 married women in the labor force, only 1,118,000 (or 18.3 percent) had children under the age of six.[51] For Updike to portray women adjusting instead of protesting does not imply endorsement of their options. As the despair he attributes to the drunken Janice indicates, it certainly does not provide evidence that women are, or should be, content with their condition.

It is easy to see these women in *Rabbit, Run* as the literary mothers of a whole slew of women who refuse to take the transcendent risk that in Updike's suburban world is the closest one gets to macho behavior, who in piercing through the pretensions of that risk at every opportunity act as the equivalent of spiritual castrators: Penny in *The Centaur* who treats Peter's mythologizing her as Philyra as evidence that he loves her only in dreams,[52] Angela in *Couples* who shrugs off Piet's designation of her genitals as "heavenly" as nothing unusual,[53] Peggy in *Of the Farm* who likens the sanctuary her mother-in-law proposes to a concentration camp.[54] Such an inability to enter into any form of transcendent thought, to remain conceptually bound to the here and now, may indicate women's imaginative limitations to an author who is devoted to a real/unreal continuum that defines God as "the union of the actual and the ideal" and, in wedding the tangible and transcendental, conceives of all things as "masks for God."[55] For such a charge to hold true, however, one must accept what in many circles has become a myth of authorial intentionality. Working with the text alone provides far less grounds for criticism because the transcendental ideal is never completely espoused in the novel. The appropriately named Doctor Crowe who, in delivering Janice's child, gets closer to the source of her womanhood than anyone else, brings back "nothing to confide, no curse, no blessing" and his eyes do not "release with thunder the mystery they have absorbed" because they witness nothing of mystery to reveal (201). With such confirmation ripping to shreds the basis on which Rabbit has constructed his sexual theology, the ersatz saint, too, falls accordingly. "You're Mr. Death himself," Ruth asserts, after which she lodges her most stinging rebuke: "You're not just nothing, you're worse than nothing" (304). With such an assessment of Rabbit's entire credo, such an inversion of all the emblems that formerly served as testaments to transcendence, the book closes. The "pure blank space" within Rabbit that had signaled his freedom shrinks to an "infinitely small" vacancy (308–9). The selfhood (not to mention sainthood) he had predicated on having a ball – in golf, in basketball, in every sense of the word – is exposed as the ultimate negation: "It's like when they heard you were great and put two men on you and no matter which way you turned you bumped into one of them and the only thing to do was pass. So you passed and the ball belonged to the others and your hands were empty and the men on you looked foolish because in effect there was nobody there'' (309). Only this time the ''nobody'' is not Odysseus in disguise, but the cyclops whose faulty vision in Updike's novel turns him into nothing but a cypher.

NOTES

1 Charles Thomas Samuels, ''The Art of Fiction XLIII: John Updike,'' *Paris Review* 45 (1968): 100.

2 John Updike, *Rabbit, Run* (1960; rev. and rpt. New York: Alfred A. Knopf, 1970), pp. 131–2. Unless otherwise noted, subsequent page references will be to the 1970 printing and will appear parenthetically after quotations.

3 John Updike, *Picked-Up Pieces* (New York: Alfred A. Knopf, 1975), p. 98; John Updike, *Rabbit at Rest* (New York: Alfred A. Knopf, 1990), p. 56.

4 See Mary Gordon, ''Good Boys and Dead Girls,'' *Good Boys and Dead Girls and Other Essays* (1991; New York: Penguin, 1992), pp. 18–20; Mary Allen, ''John Updike's Love of 'Dull Bovine Beauty,' '' *The Necessary Blankness: Women in Major American Fiction of the Sixties* (Urbana: University of Illinois Press, 1976), pp. 97–132.

5 Josephine Hendin, *Vulnerable People: A View of American Fiction Since 1945* (New York: Oxford University Press, 1978), pp. 90–91. For additional discussion of oedipal themes in Updike's work, see Gerry Brenner, ''*Rabbit, Run:* John Updike's Criticism of the 'Return to Nature,' '' *Twentieth Century Literature* 12 (1966): 5; Jack De Bellis, ''Oedipal Angstrom,'' *Wascana Review* 24.1 (1989): 45–54; Robert Detweiler, *John Updike* (Boston: Twayne, 1984), pp. 40–2; and Joyce B. Markle, *Fighters and Lovers: Theme in the Novels of John Updike* (New York: New York University Press, 1973), pp. 93–101.

6 John Updike, *Odd Jobs: Essays and Criticism* (New York: Alfred A. Knopf, 1991), p. 869.

7 John Updike, *The Centaur* (1963; New York: Fawcett Crest, 1964), p. 177. For perhaps the most explicit statement alleging Updike's presumption, see Margaret Atwood, ''Wondering What It's Like to Be a Woman,'' review of *The Witches of Eastwick,* by John Updike, *New York Times Book Review,* May 13, 1984: 40.

8 Joyce Carol Oates, "Updike's American Comedies," *Modern Fiction Studies* 21 (1975): 463, 467–8; Kathleen Verduin, "Sex, Nature, and Dualism in *The Witches of Eastwick*," *Modern Language Quarterly* 46 (1985): 308. See Verduin's excellent article, pp. 293–4, for a useful summary of feminist criticism of Updike's 1984 novel. For Updike's response to these criticisms, see Mervyn Rothstein, "In *S.*, Updike Tries the Woman's Viewpoint," *New York Times*, March 2, 1988: C-21. I am indebted to Donald J. Greiner's essay, "Body and Soul: John Updike and *The Scarlet Letter*," *Journal of Modern Literature* 15 (1989): 492–3, for calling Rothstein's article to my attention.

9 *Picked-Up Pieces*, p. 508.

10 *Odd Jobs*, p. 72.

11 John Updike, *Assorted Prose* (New York: Alfred A. Knopf, 1965), pp. 284, 285. Nearly every commentator who discusses Updike's view of male-female relations refers to his 1963 *New Yorker* essay on de Rougemont. For particularly good applications of the essay to Updike's fiction, see Robert Detweiler, "Updike's *Couples:* Eros Demythologized," *Twentieth Century Literature* 17 (1971): 237–46; and Victor Strandberg, "John Updike and the Changing of the Gods," *Mosaic* 12.1 (1978): 161–2, 170–2.

12 *Assorted Prose*, pp. 286, 287.

13 Ibid., p. 299.

14 Ibid., p. 286.

15 Ibid., p. 286.

16 D. H. Lawrence, *Women in Love* (1920; New York: Viking, 1960), p. 181; John Updike, "The Blessed Man of Boston, My Grandmother's Thimble, and Fanning Island," *Pigeon Feathers and Other Stories* (New York: Alfred A. Knopf, 1962), p. 231.

17 *Assorted Prose*, p. 284.

18 *Odd Jobs*, p. 858.

19 John Updike, *Hugging the Shore: Essays and Criticism* (New York: Alfred A. Knopf, 1983), pp. 77, 78. Donald J. Greiner bases his analysis of *A Month of Sundays, Roger's Version*, and *S.* on Updike's rejection of Hawthorne's division of body and soul. See Greiner, "Body and Soul: John Updike and *The Scarlet Letter*," pp. 475–83, for complete discussion.

20 Leslie A. Fiedler, *Love and Death in the American Novel* (1960; rev. and rpt. 1966; New York: Stein and Day, 1975), p. 26.

21 *Picked-Up Pieces*, p. 505.

22 *The Centaur*, p. 203.

23 John Updike, *Rabbit, Run* (Greenwich, CT.: Fawcett Crest, 1960), p. 70; John Updike, "Museums and Women" (1967), *Museums and Women and Other Stories* (New York: Alfred A. Knopf, 1972), p. 12; John Updike, *Couples* (New York: Alfred A. Knopf, 1968), pp. 10, 114, 422–3.

24 *Odd Jobs,* p. 71.

25 *Odd Jobs,* p. 870. See "An Interesting Emendation" (*Picked-Ip Pieces,* pp. 438–44) for Updike's discussion of the "swift secularization" of oral sex in recent American fiction and the concomitant rise of buggery in place of the "magical act" he considers fellatio to be (*Picked-Up Pieces,* p. 441).

26 Thomas Pynchon, *V.* (1963; New York: Bantam, 1964), pp. 193, 429, 434, 438; Norman Mailer, *The Prisoner of Sex* (New York: Signet-New American Library, 1971), p. 47; Norman Mailer, *The Deer Park* (1955; New York: Berkley Windhover, 1976), p. 327.

27 Joanne Dobson, "Portraits of the Lady: Imagining Women in Nineteenth-Century America," *American Literary History* 3 (1991): 396; *Odd Jobs,* pp. 67–8.

28 Gordon, p. 17; Judith Fetterley, "*An American Dream:* 'Hula, Hula,' Said the Witches," *The Resisting Reader: A Feminist Approach to American Fiction* (Bloomington: Indiana University Press, 1978), p. 158.

29 Norman Mailer, *The Presidential Papers* (1963; New York: Berkley Medallion, 1970), p. 159.

30 *Prisoner of Sex,* pp. 36, 35.

31 Ibid., p. 86.

32 Norman Mailer, *An American Dream* (1965; New York: Dell, 1970), pp. 48, 122–3.

33 *Prisoner of Sex,* p. 66.

34 *Picked-Up Pieces,* p. 504.

35 John Updike, *Rabbit Is Rich* (1981; New York: Fawcett Crest-Ballantine, 1982), pp. 392, 391.

36 *Pigeon Feathers,* p. 253.

37 *Rabbit Is Rich,* p. 209.

38 *Rabbit at Rest,* p. 111.

39 *The Centaur,* p. 184.

40 *Rabbit at Rest,* p. 461.

41 John Updike, *Rabbit Redux* (1971; New York: Fawcett Crest-Ballantine, 1972), p. 270. For discussions of the linkage between sex and money that is more obvious in *Rabbit Is Rich,* see Detweiler, *John Updike,* pp. 175–8; and Judie Newman, *John Updike* (New York: St. Martin's, 1988), pp. 61–4, 70–6.

42 See, for example, the birth of the narrator's mother in "The Blessed Man of Boston, My Grandmother's Thimble, and Fanning Island" (*Pigeon Feathers*, pp. 239–40), Harry's recollection of Nelson's birth in *Rabbit, Run* (p. 11), and the circumstances surrounding the birth of Nelson's daughter in *Rabbit Is Rich* (pp. 401–2).

43 *Rabbit Is Rich*, p. 352. Updike's connection of "paternity and death, earth and faith and cars" (*Hugging the Shore*, p. 852) is longstanding and the depiction of used bodies (both male and female) as used metal recurs in much of his fiction. For representative samples, see "Packed Dirt, Churchgoing, A Dying Cat, A Traded Car" (*Pigeon Feathers*, p. 279) and *The Centaur* (pp. 71, 162, 186). In *Rabbit Is Rich*, Nelson will inherit his father's predisposition to judge pregnant women as "[d]efective equipment" (p. 309).

44 It is in conflating Rabbit's perspective with Updike's and neglecting to consider point of view that feminist critics of the Rabbit tetralogy most often err. Joyce Carol Oates' remarks serve as an especially astute reminder against such misreadings: "the consciousness of a Rabbit Angstrom is so foreign to Updike's own that it seems at times more a point of view, a voicing of that part of the mind unfertilized by the imagination, than a coherent personality" ("Updike's American Comedies," p. 466).

45 *The Centaur*, pp. 142–3; *Couples*, p. 95.

46 See, in particular, Larry E. Taylor, *Pastoral and Anti-Pastoral Patterns in John Updike's Fiction* (Carbondale: Southern Illinois University Press, 1971), pp. 70–85; and Brenner, pp. 3–14, for detailed discussions of Updike's antipastoral theme in *Rabbit, Run*.

47 *Rabbit Is Rich*, p. 351.

48 *The Centaur*, p. 142.

49 James Joyce, *Ulysses* (1922; New York: Vintage-Random, 1961), p. 753.

50 See, in particular, the conversations that Mrs. Robinson and Joey have about Peggy in Updike's *Of the Farm* (New York: Alfred A. Knopf, 1965), pp. 43, 138–41.

51 Allen, p. 112; United States Department of Commerce, Bureau of the Census, *Historical Statistics of the United States: Colonial Times to 1970*, 2 pts. (Washington, D.C.: n.p., 1975) 1, pp. 127, 128, 134.

52 *The Centaur*, p. 183.

53 *Couples*, p. 194.

54 *Of the Farm*, p. 71.

55 Updike, *Pigeon Feathers*, p. 249; Samuels, p. 116. Even critics whose stance is not explicitly feminist consider that Updike's failure to have

women characters engage in transcendental thought signals a limitation he ascribes to women. See, for example, Bernard Schopen, "Faith, Morality, and the Novels of John Updike," *Twentieth Century Literature* 24 (1978): 533–4.

Notes on Contributors

Eric Kielland-Lund is Associate Professor of American Literature at the University of Oslo, Norway. In addition to essays on Robert Frost, Ernest Hemingway, and Alice Walker, he is the author of *Encountering Literature* and has pioneered the first course in American popular culture in Norwegian universities.

Stacey Olster, Associate Professor of English at the State University of New York at Stony Brook, has written widely on modern American writers, among them Ann Beattie, Norman Mailer, Thomas Pynchon, and Nathanael West. She is the author of *Reminiscence and Re-Creation in Contemporary American Fiction.*

Sanford Pinsker, Shadek Professor of Humanities at Franklin and Marshall College, is a prolific book reviewer, literary essayist, critic, and poet whose work includes studies of Joseph Conrad, Philip Roth, Cynthia Ozick, and Joseph Heller. He is the author of *Between Two Worlds: The American Novel in the 1960's* and *Bearing the Bad News: Contemporary American Literature and Culture,* and serves as co-editor of *Holocaust Studies Annual.*

Philip Stevick, Professor of English at Temple University, has published *Alternative Pleasures: Postrealist Fiction and the Tradition* and *The Chapter in Fiction: Theories of Narrative Division.* He edited *The Theory of the Novel* and *AntiStory: An Anthology of Experimental Fiction.*

Stanley Trachtenberg is Professor of American Literature at Texas Christian University. Formerly a senior editor at Macmillan and at Crown, he has edited books on Saul Bellow, John Hawkes, and on postmodernism in several disciplines and is the author of *Understanding Donald Barthelme.*

Selected Bibliography

Each of the four essays in this collection refers to the 1960 Knopf edition of *Rabbit, Run* as revised in the 1970 reprint. In addition to the books and articles listed here, useful comments on *Rabbit, Run* may be found throughout the many interviews John Updike has granted as well as in his own writing. References to several of the most important of these sources are contained in the notes to this volume.

Ahearn, Kerry. "Family and Adultery: Images and Ideas in John Updike's Rabbit Novels." *Twentieth Century Literature* 34 (1988): 62–83.

Borgman, Paul. "The Tragic Hero of Updike's *Rabbit, Run.*" *Renascence* 29 (Winter 1977): 111–17.

Brenner, Gerry. "Rabbit Run: John Updike's Criticism of Nature." *Twentieth Century Literature* 12 (1966): 3–14.

Burhans, Clinton S. Jr. "Things Falling Apart: Structure and Theme in *Rabbit, Run.*" *Studies in the Novel* 5 (1973): 336–51.

De Bellis, Jack. "Oedipal Angstrom." *Wascana Review* 24 (1989): 435–59.

Detweiler, Robert. "John Updike and the Indictment of Culture-Protestantism." *Four Spiritual Crises in Mid-Century American Fiction.* Gainesville: University of Florida Press, 1963: 14–24.

"*Rabbit, Run:* The Quest for a Vanished Grail." *John Updike,* rev. ed. Boston: G. K. Hall, 1984: 33–45.

Doner, Dean. "Rabbit Angstrom's Unseen World." *New World Writing* 20. Philadelphia: Lippincott, 1962: 62–75

Galloway, David. *The Absurd Hero in American Fiction.* Austin: University of Texas Press, rev. ed. 1981.

Greiner, Donald J. *John Updike's Novels.* Athens: Ohio University Press, 1983: 47–63.

Hallissy, Margaret. "Updike's *Rabbit, Run* and Pascal's *Pensées. Christianity and Literature* 30 (1981): 25–32.

Hamilton, Alice, and Kenneth Hamilton. *The Elements of John Updike.* Grand Rapids, Michigan: William B. Eerdmans, 1970, pp. 137–55.

Horvath, Brooke. "The Failure of Erotic Questing in John Updike's Rabbit Novels." *Denver Quartery 23* (1988): 70–89.

Markle, Joyce. "*Rabbit, Run:* The Self-Centered Lover." *Fighters and Lovers: Theme in the Novels of John Updike.* New York: New York University Press, 1973: 37–60.

Neary, John M. " 'Ah: Runs': Updike, Rabbit, and Repetition." *Religion and Literature* 21 (1989): 89–110.

Ristoff, Dilvio. *Updike's America: The Presence of Contemporary American History in John Updike's Rabbit Trilogy.* New York: Lang, 1988.

Schopen, Bernard A. "Faith, Morality, and the Novels of John Updike." *Twentieth Century Literature* 24 (1978): 523–35.

Siegel, Gary. "Rabbit Runs Down." *The Modern American Novel and the Movies,* ed. Gerald Peary and Roger Shatzkin. New York: Ungar, 1978, pp. 247–55.

Standley, Fred. "*Rabbit, Run:* An Image of Life." *Midwest Quarterly* 8 (Summer 1967): 371–86.

Stubbs, John C. "The Search for Perfection in *Rabbit, Run.*" *Critique: Studies in Modern Fiction* 10 (Spring/Summer 1968): 94–101.

Suderman, Elmer. "The Right Way and the Good Way in *Rabbit, Run.*" *University Review* 36 (Autumn 1969): 13–21.

Taylor, Larry. "*Rabbit, Run:* An Anti-Pastoral Satire." *Pastoral and Anti-Pastoral Patterns in John Updike's Fiction.* Carbondale: Southern Illinois University Press, 1971, pp. 70–85.

Vargo, Edward P. "The Magic Dance: *Rabbit, Run.*" *Rainstorms and Fire: Ritual in the Novels of John Updike.* Port Washington, NY: Kennikat Press, 1973, pp. 51–80.

Waldmeir, Joseph. "It's the Going That's Important, Not the Getting There: Rabbit's Questing Non-Quest." *Modern Fiction Studies* 20 (Spring 1974): 13–27.

Waldron, Randall. "Rabbit Revised." *American Literature* 56 (1984): 51–67.

Wilson, Matthew. "The Rabbit Tetralogy: From Solitude to Society to Solitude Again." *Modern Fiction Studies* 37 (Spring 1991): 5–24.

Wright, Derek. "Mapless Motion: Form and Space in Updike's *Rabbit Run.*" *Modern Fiction Studies* 37 (Spring 1991): 35–44.